Lost Gateway to Manifestation

The Forbidden Frequency Method to Align Your Energy and Reshape Reality

Codex Occulto

© **Copyright 2025 by Codex Occulto - All rights reserved.**

This publication provides accurate and reliable information on the subject matter discussed. It is sold with the understanding that the publisher is not offering legal, accounting, or professional services. For such advice, consult a qualified expert.

No part of this document may be copied, reproduced, stored, or shared—electronically or in print—without written permission from the publisher. All rights reserved.

The content is presented as-is, with no guarantees. The publisher assumes no responsibility for any loss, damage, or consequences resulting from the use or misuse of the information provided.

Trademarks mentioned are the property of their respective owners and are used for identification purposes only. This publication is not affiliated with them.

All copyrights remain with their respective authors unless held by the publisher.

ISBN: 979-8-89965-373-5

Imprint: Staten House

Staten House

Table of Contents

The Key Was Never Lost—You Were Just Never Shown It	7
Chapter 1: The Forgotten Laws Beyond Attraction	**13**
Chapter 2: Ancient Manifestation Rituals from Egypt to Atlantis	**17**
Egypt: The Science of the Sacred Word	17
Atlantis: The Crystalline Codex	18
Greece: The Mysteries of Eleusis	18
India: Mantra and Mudra	19
Mesoamerica: Calendar and Cosmic Timing	19
The Common Threads	20
Chapter 3: Why Modern Manifestation Doesn't Work	**21**
The Flaws of Modern Manifestation	21
So What Works?	23
Chapter 4: The Gateway Myth Across Cultures	**26**
The Veil in Mystical Traditions	26
The Third Eye: The Inner Portal	27
Axis Mundi: The World Tree and the Center of All	28
The Egyptian Duat and the Journey of the Soul	28
The Cave, the Labyrinth, and the Door	29
Why This Matters	30
Stepping Into the Inner Gateway	30
Chapter 5: The Anatomy of the Inner Portal	**35**
The Mind: Interface, Narrative, and Gatekeeper	35
Emotion: The Frequency, the Feedback, and the Fuel	37
Intention: The Blueprint of Creation	38
Energy: The Field That Responds to You	39
Putting It All Together: A Living Portal	40
Chapter 6: How Trauma Blocks the Gateway	**42**
The Physiology of a Blocked Gateway	42
Energetic Memory and the Subconscious	43
Trauma as Disconnection from the Self	43
The Illusion of the "High Vibe Only" Culture	43
Unfreezing the Energy	44
Rewriting the Trauma Script	44

From Wound to Wisdom	45
Chapter 7: Activation Through Shadow Work	**47**
The Nature of the Shadow	47
How Shadow Work Supports Manifestation	48
The Three Faces of the Shadow	48
Common Shadow Beliefs That Sabotage Manifestation	48
How to Begin Shadow Work	49
Signs Your Shadow Is Integrating	50
Chapter 8: The Role of the Heart Field	**52**
The Heart: Science Meets Spirit	52
Heart Coherence: The Missing Ingredient	52
The Heart as Portal	53
Why the Heart Is Crucial for Manifestation	53
How to Cultivate Heart Coherence	54
The Role of the Heart in Shadow and Healing	55
Signs Your Heart Field Is Activated	55
The Heart-Field Connection to the Quantum	55
Chapter 9: Energy Alignment in 3 Levels: Body, Mind, Spirit	**61**
Level 1: The Body – The Vessel of Vibration	61
Level 2: The Mind – The Narrative Maker	62
Level 3: The Spirit – The Frequency Keeper	63
The Harmony of All Three	64
Chapter 10: Rituals to Open the Gateway Daily	**66**
Morning Gateway Activation: 10 Minutes to Set Your Field	66
Evening Gateway Activation: 10 Minutes to Integrate and Release	67
Optional Enhancers to Deepen Your Rituals	68
Creating Your Gateway Ritual	68
Chapter 11: Dreamwork and Hypnagogic Manifestation	**70**
What Is the Hypnagogic State?	70
Why Dreamwork Supports Manifestation	71
Step 1: Preparing for Hypnagogic Manifestation	71
Step 2: Dream Journaling and Interpretation	72
Step 3: Hypnagogic Imprinting Techniques	73
Step 4: Lucid Dreaming and Advanced Practice	74

Bringing It All Together 75

Chapter 12: The Sacred Delay: Why It Hasn't Shown Up Yet **76**

You're Being Calibrated to the Frequency 76

Your Timeline Isn't the Universe's Timeline 77

You're Being Asked to Deepen the Signal 77

Your Attachment Is Creating Resistance 77

There Are Still Lessons Unfolding 78

Your Growth Is the Real Manifestation 78

Chapter 13: Living as a Gateway Keeper **84**

The Frequency Comes First 84

Energetic Integrity Becomes Your Compass 85

You Create Everything 85

You Hold the Field No Matter What 86

You Become a Beacon 86

You Manifest Without Forcing 86

Chapter 14: Manifesting with Words, Movement, and Art **88**

Words as Spells 88

Movement as Energy Shifter 89

Art as Portal 90

Sound and Voice as Frequency 90

Living as a Creative Channel 91

Chapter 15: Sacred Sexual Energy & Manifestation **92**

Understanding the Creative Fire 92

Clearing Shame and Reclaiming Sovereignty 93

Solo Practice for Manifestation 93

Partner Practice for Amplification 94

The Orgasmic State as Gateway 95

Living in Turn-On 95

The Sacred Integration 96

Chapter 16: Relationships & Collective Reality Creation **98**

Understanding the Shared Field 98

Co-Creation in Romantic Partnership 99

Healing and Rewriting Old Templates 100

Energetic Hygiene in Relationships 101

The Planetary Field	101
Chapter 17: Synchronicity as the New GPS	**106**
How Synchronicity Works	106
Learning to Listen	107
Following the Threads	107
Signs vs. Tests	108
Synchronicity as a Mirror	108
Collaborating with the Field	109
When Synchronicity Fades	109
Synchronicity and Divine Timing	109
Chapter 18: The Spiral Path: Recoding Your Identity	**111**
Who Are You Becoming?	111
The Old Code Must Be Seen to Be Rewritten	112
The Body Remembers	113
Repetition Creates Reality	113
Hold Compassion Through the Spiral	114
The Self as Ceremony	114
Chapter 19: Rewriting the Script of Reality	**115**
The Reality Mirror	115
Belief as Creative Code	115
Emotional Resonance	116
The Power of Language	116
Ritualizing the Rewrite	117
Letting Go of the Old Script	118
Reinforcing the Field	118
You Are the Author	118
Chapter 20: The Real Secret: You Were the Gateway All Along	**120**
Awakening the Inner Creator	120
Living From Essence	121
Your Frequency Is the Offering	121
You're No Longer Waiting	122
No More Gatekeepers	122
Manifestation Is a Way of Being	122
You Are the Miracle	123

The Key Was Never Lost—You Were Just Never Shown It

There is a gateway.

It is not made of wood or stone. It cannot be unlocked by keys forged in metal. It lives within you, ancient and alive, pulsing just beneath the surface of your awareness. Every time you've longed for more—more freedom, more alignment, more magic—you've brushed against its edge. And every time you were told to "just think positive and let go," a door that should have opened... remained shut.

Not because you failed. Not because you weren't worthy. But because you were never given the full map.

This book is not about selling your hope wrapped in pretty language. This is about initiation—into a deeper understanding of who you are and what you're truly capable of. It is about remembering that the act of creation is not something you *do*, it is something you *are*.

Manifestation is not a vision board. It's not a wish list for the universe. It is a dynamic, living interaction between your inner world and the field around you.

But something has been lost. Not in the way of vanishing, but in the way of forgetting. Ancient civilizations knew the laws of the unseen. They danced with energy, spoke to the quantum field with clarity, and shaped their realities with intention, ritual, and coherence. From the temples of Egypt to the stories of Atlantis, from Vedic texts to the tribal songs of Indigenous elders, the same pattern reappears: there is a bridge between the formless and the formed. A gateway.

You were born with it. But no one taught you how to find it.

Until now.

This is not a gentle walk through positive affirmations. This is a deep dive into the codes of manifestation long buried beneath spiritual trends and social media mantras. Here, we will unravel the forgotten laws, resurrect the rituals, and awaken the energetic blueprint within you.

This book will challenge what you think you know. It will ask you to go deeper than your mindset. It will invite you to meet yourself beyond the roles, beyond the wounds, beyond the surface. Because only there—in the still, sovereign space within—can the gateway open.

This is for the seekers. The ones who feel the pull. The ones who know, in their bones, that magic is real and power is personal.

The key was never lost. You were just never shown it.

PART I: THE LOST WISDOM

Chapter 1: The Forgotten Laws Beyond Attraction

For decades, the Law of Attraction has been marketed as the master key to manifestation: think it, feel it, believe it, and it will come. While this concept awakened millions to the idea that thought influences reality, it left behind a deeper, more ancient understanding—one that mystics, alchemists, and wisdom keepers have always known. The Law of Attraction is not the whole story. It is only a fragment of a much older framework, one composed of multiple laws, each governing a different layer of reality.

When you only work with the Law of Attraction, you're using a single brushstroke to paint a multidimensional masterpiece. The result is often frustration, inconsistency, or partial results. You may wonder why you're "doing everything right" and still not seeing the life you desire to materialize. The reason is simple: you're not working with the full architecture of creation. You're not engaging with the full set of laws.

These laws are not dogma. They are energetic principles—patterns of truth observed and recorded across time by those who studied the structure of reality. They are found in Hermeticism, Taoism, and alchemical traditions, and even encoded in myth. They describe not just how to attract, but how to align, balance, and evolve.

Let us explore seven of these often-forgotten laws and understand how they shape, direct, and determine the quality of what you manifest.

1. **The Law of Mentalism**: All is Mind Everything begins in consciousness. The universe is mental, shaped by thought, perception, and awareness. Your external world is an echo of your inner world. But this law goes deeper than simply "think positive." It reveals that reality itself is a projection of your consciousness. To change your world, you must change your mind—not just

your surface thoughts, but your core beliefs, your hidden assumptions, your definitions of self, others, and life itself.

When you internalize this law, you stop blaming external conditions. You realize that the root of every experience lies within you. Not as a punishment, but as empowerment.

2. **The Law of Correspondence**: As Within, So Without This law teaches that the microcosm reflects the macrocosm. Your inner environment mirrors your outer reality, and vice versa. Your body reflects your thoughts. Your relationships reflect your subconscious programming. Your physical surroundings mirror your energetic patterns.

To shift your outer world, start by examining the stories you're carrying inside. If chaos surrounds you, where is there disorder within? If love is missing, how have you blocked love from yourself? As within, so without.

3. **The Law of Vibration**: Everything Moves Nothing is truly still. Everything in the universe is in a state of vibration—thoughts, emotions, matter, even so-called space. Your vibration is the total of your dominant thoughts, emotional set points, subconscious beliefs, and energetic tone.

Manifestation occurs when your vibration aligns with the frequency of your desire. But vibration isn't something you fake. You can't slap a high-vibe affirmation on top of unresolved grief or rage and expect coherence. Your true vibration is shaped by your integration, not your performance.

4. **The Law of Polarity**: Everything Has Its Opposite Light and Shadow. Expansion and contraction. Joy and pain. The Law of Polarity teaches us that everything contains its opposite, and transformation occurs by working with contrast, not denying it. This law is often misunderstood in the manifestation world, where people avoid discomfort or negative emotions.

But in truth, your pain holds the seed of your power. Your fear reveals your next threshold. To transmute limitation, you must not reject it—you must witness and work with it. Every polarity is a portal.

5. **The Law of Rhythm**: All Things Rise and Fall Nature moves in cycles: the tides, the moon, and the seasons. Your energy, emotions, and manifestations move in rhythm too. There are times of expansion and times of rest. Times of blooming and times of compost.

When you forget this law, you fight the natural flow. You try to force results in winter or resist slowing down when the rhythm asks you to reflect. By aligning with your inner and outer seasons, you move with grace, not force. You trust divine timing.

6. **The Law of Cause and Effect**: Nothing Happens by Chance Every thought, word, and action sends a ripple into the field. There are no random events—only results of energetic causes, whether seen or unseen. Manifestation is not magic; it's mechanics. You are always planting seeds with your energy, and the harvest reflects what you've sown.

This law is empowering. It reminds you that you are not a victim of fate—you are a creator, constantly generating effects through your vibration and choices.

7. **The Law of Gender**: The Masculine and Feminine Principles This law has nothing to do with biological sex and everything to do with polarity. The Law of Gender speaks to the balance of masculine and feminine energies within all things: action and receptivity, logic and intuition, doing and being.

Many manifestation practices are overly masculine—focused on control, action, and strategy. Others swing too far into the feminine—focused solely on receiving without direction. True creation comes from the union of both. The inner masculine sets the container, the inner feminine fills it with life.

Reclaiming the Full Formula These laws are not abstract theories. They are living dynamics, operating in your life whether you acknowledge them or not. When you align with them, you become a conscious creator. You stop working against the current. You begin to surf the waves of reality with awareness and intention.

This is why many people struggle with manifestation. They are trying to build castles in the sky with only one tool. The Law of Attraction may help you dream, but these laws help you build.

To unlock the full gateway to manifestation, you must integrate these principles—not just in your mind, but in your being. This is the difference between wishing and embodying. Between temporary results and lasting transformation.

You don't just attract what you want. You attract what you are. And what you are is shaped by what you understand, what you believe, and how you align with the deeper laws of creation.

Chapter 2: Ancient Manifestation Rituals from Egypt to Atlantis

Long before manifestation was reduced to vision boards and daily affirmations, ancient civilizations worked with energy, frequency, and the unseen realms through precise and sacred rituals. These cultures were not primitive. They were repositories of advanced knowledge—keepers of metaphysical systems that merged spiritual insight with natural law.

They didn't just speak about manifestation. They *lived* it. In their temples, ceremonies, and mystery schools, they encoded techniques for aligning human intention with cosmic intelligence.

Egypt: The Science of the Sacred Word

Ancient Egypt held one of the most advanced systems of metaphysical knowledge the world has ever known. The temples of Luxor, Karnak, and Edfu were not just places of worship—they were energetic technologies.

Egyptian manifestation rituals centered around *hekau*—sacred words of power. These weren't ordinary speech. Hekau was the deliberate use of sound, symbol, and intention to affect reality. Words were vibrational codes, and to speak them was to activate creation.

Priests and priestesses would:

- Chant sacred names to align with divine archetypes
- Inscribe symbols (like the Ankh, Djed, and Eye of Horus) onto temple walls as frequency transmitters
- Perform breath control and visualization to anchor intention into the Ka

(energetic double) and Ba (soul essence)

Every gesture, every sound, every glyph was intentional. Nothing was random. Egypt taught that manifestation required purity of heart, clarity of mind, and resonance between the seen and unseen.

Atlantis: The Crystalline Codex

Though largely lost to legend, Atlantis persists in memory and myth because it encoded a high-frequency civilization deeply attuned to energetic laws. Atlanteans reportedly used crystal technology, harmonic resonance, and mental discipline to co-create with universal energies.

Manifestation in Atlantis was taught as a path of mastery. Citizens were trained in temples of initiation, learning to align their frequency with the desired outcome, not through force but through coherence.

Practices likely included:

- Meditating with crystals to tune to specific intentions
- Using sound frequencies to restructure water and matter
- Harnessing sexual energy not for pleasure alone, but as a creative fuel
- Creating architectural forms (pyramids, domes) that amplified intention

Their downfall, as told in esoteric sources, came when this sacred science was corrupted—used for control instead of harmony. Their story reminds us that power without wisdom leads to destruction.

Greece: The Mysteries of Eleusis

In Ancient Greece, manifestation took a more initiatory path. At Eleusis, for over 2,000 years, participants underwent the Eleusinian Mysteries—a series of sacred rites centered around death, rebirth, and divine union.

Though much remains secret, the core idea was that the transformation of the self *preceded* the transformation of reality. Initiates would descend into darkness (both literal and symbolic), face their fears, and emerge with new awareness.

This echoes the truth that many miss: manifestation is not about avoiding darkness, but integrating it. True creation comes when the unconscious is made conscious—when shadow and light unite.

India: Mantra and Mudra

Ancient Vedic traditions offer perhaps the most accessible and enduring manifestation rituals today: mantra (sacred sound) and mudra (sacred gesture).

Mantras are vibrational codes. Repeating a mantra like "Om Namah Shivaya" or "So Hum" activates specific states of consciousness. Mantras tune your mind and body to the frequency of your desired state—peace, clarity, abundance.

Mudras are symbolic hand gestures that direct energy through the body's meridian system. Used in combination with breath and intention, they create a loop of focused energy.

These practices teach that the body is not separate from the spirit. That physical form can direct metaphysical flow. That stillness and sound together create reality.

Mesoamerica: Calendar and Cosmic Timing

The Mayans and Aztecs understood that manifestation worked in harmony with celestial cycles. Their calendars, particularly the Tzolk'in, weren't just timekeeping tools—they were energetic maps.

Each day carried its vibration. Rituals were timed to match specific energetic signatures. The manifestation wasn't random—it was rhythmic. This teaches us that timing isn't just luck. It's alignment.

Modern manifestation often ignores divine timing, leading to frustration. Ancient Mesoamerica reminds us: that when you plant at the right moment, nature does the work.

The Common Threads

Across all these cultures, several core principles repeat:

- Manifestation is sacred. It's not a trick, but a communion.

- Sound, symbol, and movement matter. They carry frequency.

- Alignment with natural cycles is essential. You're part of something larger.

- The self must be purified. Shadow work and integrity are prerequisites.

This ancient wisdom was never about getting more—it was about *becoming* more. The rituals were mirrors for transformation, inviting the practitioner to evolve into the version of themselves capable of holding the reality they desired.

Chapter 3: Why Modern Manifestation Doesn't Work

If you've ever tried to manifest something—a relationship, a career breakthrough, a dream home—you've probably encountered this moment: the high of hopeful energy followed by the slow erosion of belief. Weeks go by. Nothing shifts. Maybe you meditate harder, journal longer, or repeat affirmations more intensely. Yet still, the desired result doesn't come.

The typical reaction? You blame yourself.

You're told you must not want it enough. Or you're "blocking it with your doubt." Or worst of all: "You're not in alignment."

But what if the issue isn't you? What if the modern manifestation model itself is flawed?

The popular teachings of manifestation tend to be rooted in half-truths: attractive enough to go viral, but hollow enough to leave you frustrated. The mainstream method reduces manifestation to a three-step formula: think positive, visualize, and let go. While these steps *contain* slivers of truth, they leave out essential dimensions of the process—especially the shadow, the body, and the unconscious.

The Flaws of Modern Manifestation

Let's examine where the common approach breaks down:

1. It Ignores the Unconscious Mind The conscious mind represents only a small fraction of our total mental activity. Neuroscience suggests that up to 95% of our behavior is governed by unconscious programming. This includes beliefs about money, love, self-worth, and power—many of which were formed in early childhood or inherited epigenetically.

If you consciously affirm abundance but unconsciously associate wealth with guilt, betrayal, or danger, your energy will transmit a mixed signal. The field responds to frequency, not words. Until you excavate and integrate these buried beliefs, your manifestations will be blocked at the root.

2. It Bypasses Emotional Energy Emotions are energetic signatures. They inform your vibrational output. Yet modern methods often encourage you to suppress "negative" emotions in favor of positivity. This creates inner fragmentation. Instead of wholeness, you cultivate performance—pretending to be high-vibe while quietly carrying shame, grief, or anger.

True manifestation requires *emotional coherence*—the alignment between your thoughts, feelings, and energy. Repressed emotion creates static in the field. That's why shadow work isn't optional—it's foundational.

3. It Disregards the Body Your body is not a passive container. It is an electromagnetic generator. HeartMath Institute research has shown that the heart's electromagnetic field is 5,000 times stronger than the brain's. Your posture, breath patterns, and muscle memory all carry energetic codes that either harmonize or disrupt your intention.

You can't manifest from the neck up. If your body feels unsafe, unworthy, or frozen in trauma response, no amount of mental visualization will override that state. True manifestation must be embodied.

4. It Simplifies the Quantum Field The Law of Attraction has been oversimplified to the point of distortion. The idea that "like attracts like" is a partial truth. The quantum field responds to coherence, not just similarity. You can desire something and still repel it if your frequency is scattered, conflicted, or incongruent.

Moreover, manifestation is *nonlinear*. The shortest path between desire and reality is not always direct. The field rearranges your circumstances in ways that often challenge your ego or require deep internal shifts before the external appears.

5. It Encourages Magical Thinking Without Sacred Discipline There's a difference between faith and fantasy. Mainstream manifestation encourages people to wish without work and to want without initiation. But true manifestation is a path of becoming. It asks you to evolve into the version of yourself who naturally lives in the reality you're calling in.

This requires practice. Presence. Ritual. Not as punishment—but as energetic anchoring. Without a sacred container, your intention floats like a balloon without a string: directionless.

6. It Emphasizes the Outcome Modern manifestation is obsessed with *getting*—more money, the perfect partner, and the dream house. While desire is natural and beautiful, fixation on outcome often pulls you out of presence and into lack. Ironically, the more you chase a desire from emptiness, the more you reinforce its absence.

Ancient traditions knew this. They understood that creation flows best from abundance, not deficiency—from a state of overflow, not need. When you *become* the source, manifestation becomes magnetic.

So What Works?

If the old model is broken, what replaces it? The answer isn't a trendy hack or a rebranded affirmation ritual. It's not another external tool promising instant results. What replaces the old model is a return to wholeness—a deep, embodied remembrance of who you really are and how reality truly works.

Real manifestation is not a mental exercise or a moment of luck. It is **energetic stewardship**. It's the conscious and continuous alignment of your mind, body, emotions, and soul—all operating as one coherent system—acting in harmony with a vision that doesn't just serve your ego, but elevates your entire being and contributes to the evolution of the whole.

This kind of creation is not accidental. It is initiated, nurtured, and sustained through the following pillars:

- **Inner work to release limiting programs.** These are the inherited scripts and unconscious beliefs that distort your signal. When you identify and dismantle them, you reclaim your power to choose new patterns.

- **Emotional regulation to create coherence.** Your emotions are not barriers; they are indicators. When you learn to move through them with grace instead of suppression, you open a field of clarity and magnetic resonance.

- **Embodiment practices to anchor your signal.** Thought alone is not enough. The body must live the frequency. Through breathwork, movement, and somatic awareness, you stabilize your vibration and become a living transmission of your desired reality.

- **Aligned action to interface with the material world.** Energy flows into matter through consistent, inspired action. When your steps mirror your inner knowing, the world begins to mirror your inner transformation.

- **Trust in the timing and intelligence of the field.** Manifestation doesn't obey human impatience. It follows universal intelligence. Surrender is not giving up—it's aligning with something greater than your limited perception.

This path is not about bypassing difficulty. On the contrary—it's about becoming powerful within the storms. Real manifestation requires emotional maturity, energetic discipline, and a willingness to feel your way through the fog. Creation happens when you meet your discomfort not with avoidance, but with presence.

It's not about waiting. It's about **resonating**. Waiting implies passivity, hoping something will change while you stay the same. Resonance implies transformation. It means becoming the vibrational match to the experience you desire—right now.

It's not about forcing outcomes. It's about **becoming the person who naturally lives**

in the reality you once only imagined. When your internal frequency changes, your external experience is compelled to shift. Reality doesn't respond to what you want—it responds to what you are.

You are not here to wish. You are here to **create**. To sculpt reality with your frequency, your choices, and your devotion to what's possible.

And that creation begins when you step beyond the surface of thought, into the deeper layers of your being—into the hidden dimensions where beliefs are born, where patterns are seeded, where your soul communicates in symbols and sensations. This is where all true magic lives—not in the intellect, but in the integrated field of your total self.

You are the tuning fork. You are the transmitter. You are the portal.

This is not new knowledge—it is ancient, encoded in your cells, in your breath, in your longing. You are not learning something foreign. You are remembering what was once natural.

Chapter 4: The Gateway Myth Across Cultures

The idea of a mystical gateway—a portal to higher knowledge, inner transformation, and unseen realities—is not new. It is as old as humanity itself. Across time and space, cultures separated by oceans and languages described a similar archetype: a threshold that connects the material and spiritual realms. This is no coincidence. It is evidence of a shared intuitive knowing, a collective memory embedded deep within our consciousness.

These gateways are not mere metaphors. They are energetic realities. They describe experiences, thresholds, and turning points where consciousness expands and a new layer of reality becomes accessible. The veil lifts, the vision sharpens, and the old self begins to dissolve.

From the Third Eye of the East to the Veil of the Mystics, from the Tree of Life in Kabbalah to the Axis Mundi of the shamans, the message is consistent: there is more to reality than meets the eye—and there is a way to access it.

The Veil in Mystical Traditions

Many esoteric teachings speak of a veil—a thin energetic barrier that separates the seen from the unseen. In Western mysticism, the Veil of Parokhet in the ancient Jewish temple separated the Holy of Holies from the rest of the world. It was said that only the High Priest could pass through it, and only under strict ritual conditions.

In Christian mysticism, the tearing of the temple veil at the crucifixion symbolized the removal of separation between humanity and the divine. In Gnostic texts, the veil is often described as illusion, Maya, or ignorance—a distortion that prevents us from perceiving truth.

In all these cases, the veil is not a physical thing. It is a state of consciousness. It is the fog of conditioning, the blindness of fear, the static of trauma. To pierce it is not to travel somewhere far, but to awaken to what has always been present—just beyond the edge of your habitual awareness.

To walk through the veil is to return to clarity. It is a passage not through space, but through perception.

The Third Eye: The Inner Portal

In Hindu and Buddhist traditions, the Third Eye (or Ajna chakra) is the seat of insight and perception beyond ordinary vision. Located between the eyebrows, this energetic center is said to govern intuition, clarity, and spiritual sight. Yogis and mystics have trained for years to activate this center through meditation, breathwork, mantras, and discipline.

The Third Eye is often called the "eye of wisdom"—a faculty that perceives beyond illusion. It doesn't see with the physical eyes; it sees with the soul. It's the part of you that recognizes truth by resonance, not logic.

The pineal gland—an actual gland in the center of the brain—has long been considered the biological counterpart of the Third Eye. Ancient Egyptians revered it in the form of the Eye of Horus, a symbol encoded in temple carvings that mirrors the structure of the pineal gland.

Why is this important for manifestation? Because the Third Eye is a gateway to the imaginal realm—the subtle but potent dimension where thought, symbol, and intention become energetically real. When opened and attuned, it becomes a transmitter and receiver between your consciousness and the larger field.

It is through this portal that vision becomes vibration. And vibration, when stabilized, becomes reality.

Axis Mundi: The World Tree and the Center of All

In many indigenous and shamanic cultures, there exists the concept of the Axis Mundi—the world axis or central pillar that connects the heavens, the earth, and the underworld. It is the shaman's path through the realms, the conduit through which one travels during trance, vision quest, or ritual.

In Norse mythology, it is Yggdrasil, the sacred tree whose branches reach the heavens and roots burrow into the depths. In Mesoamerican cosmology, the Ceiba tree serves a similar purpose. In Siberian and Mongolian traditions, the shaman climbs the World Tree to access knowledge, healing, and spiritual guidance.

The Axis Mundi is not just a sacred myth—it is a map of your inner structure. Your spine is a vertical line between heaven and earth. Your breath is the rhythm that carries you between states. The more attuned you become, the more you realize: that you are the World Tree. You are the bridge.

To access the Axis Mundi is to recognize that your consciousness spans realms. That your dreams, intuitions, and rituals are not escapes from reality, but deeper immersions into it.

The Egyptian Duat and the Journey of the Soul

In Egyptian cosmology, the Duat was the realm the soul traveled through after death, passing gates, guardians, and trials before reaching the afterlife. But the Duat was more than a post-mortem mythology—it was also a metaphor for inner transformation. Initiates in Egyptian temples underwent symbolic death and rebirth as part of their training.

Each gate of the Duat required the initiate to speak truth, face shadow, and align with divine order (Ma'at). The judgment of the heart was not about moralism—it was about frequency. If the heart was heavier than the feather of truth, the soul was not ready to ascend.

This mirrors what happens in manifestation: your desires must pass through layers of internal distortion—doubt, fear, conditioning—before they can take form. You are not punished by the universe; you are purified by the process.

The Cave, the Labyrinth, and the Door

Throughout myth and mysticism, we find recurring imagery: the dark cave (Plato), the labyrinth (Crete), and the hidden door (fairy tales). These are not just story devices—they are maps of the inner world.

The cave represents retreat, introspection, and the descent into the unconscious. It is the womb of transformation, where vision is born in darkness.

The labyrinth is the path of confusion, ego, and trial. It is the pattern of misdirection you must navigate to find your center.

The door is the final threshold—the moment of choice. Will you stay in the familiar, or step into the unknown? Will you cling to your old identity, or embrace the becoming?

These motifs are powerful because they reflect real psychological and energetic experiences. When you begin to manifest consciously, you are entering the labyrinth, confronting the dragon, and finding the key. And at every turn, you are being asked: Who are you now?

Why This Matters

Why do so many cultures, so many traditions, point to the same idea of a gateway? Because it is real. Because it is archetypal. Because it is encoded into the structure of the human journey.

But here's the twist: the gateway is not out there. It's in you.

You are the temple and the priestess. You are the guardian and the traveler. You are the veil and the one who lifts it.

All of these traditions—Eastern, Western, indigenous, mystical—are ultimately pointing you back to the same truth: **You are the portal.**

The symbols, rituals, and myths are keys—not the treasure itself. The treasure is your activated, aligned, and awakened self. When you recognize this, the myths no longer feel like stories of others. They become the living map of your inner transformation.

Stepping Into the Inner Gateway

In the next part of the book, we'll leave behind the ancient maps and turn inward. You've seen the signs. You've held the symbols. Now it's time to become the temple itself.

To do that, you'll need to understand the anatomy of your inner gateway—the architecture of consciousness that determines what you create, what you receive, and what you still resist.

We're not chasing magic. We're becoming it.

Part II: The Gateway Within

Chapter 5: The Anatomy of the Inner Portal

To open the gateway to true manifestation, we must turn inward. This isn't just poetic language—it's a literal return to the multidimensional structure of your inner self. The ancient traditions we've explored all point to the same essential truth: your ability to shape reality does not originate in the outside world. It begins—and ends—in your inner coherence.

The world around you reflects the world within you. What you see, experience, and attract is not arbitrary; it is a mirror of your current alignment. This is why two people can live in the same city, have similar resources, and walk through radically different realities—because their internal landscapes are broadcasting completely different frequencies.

To unlock your power as a creator, you must understand the architecture of this inner world. Like any sacred technology, your inner portal has a design, and it responds best when understood, respected, and maintained.

This chapter maps the anatomy of that portal—the four foundational components that determine your vibration, perception, and creative ability. These elements are: **Mind, Emotion, Intention, and Energy.**

Each one is a portal in itself. But when they work together, they create a powerful inner alignment that activates the gateway to conscious manifestation.

The Mind: Interface, Narrative, and Gatekeeper

Your mind is not just a thinking machine. It's the interface between your internal experience and external perception. It interprets, filters, narrates, and assigns meaning to everything you encounter. But most importantly, it is **programmable**—by repetition, trauma, education, culture, or conscious re-patterning.

What you believe, you perceive. And what you consistently perceive, you begin to expect and receive. Beliefs are not passive—they're active templates projected onto the quantum field. If your mind is saturated with scarcity, even abundance will feel threatening. If you believe you're unworthy of love, you will subconsciously reject or sabotage every opportunity for it.

Most people's minds are running on autopilot, governed by loops of inherited and unexamined narratives:

- "I always have to work hard for everything."
- "People can't be trusted."
- "I'm too late. It's too late."

These mental scripts are not just thoughts. They are **energetic commands**. They quietly shape your frequency and limit what your subconscious mind allows into your field.

The conscious mind can set the goal, but it's the **subconscious mind that drives the vehicle**. And this is why affirmations alone often fail. If the subconscious is running a conflicting program, it will override the conscious input every time.

To reprogram the mind effectively, you must:

- Identify limiting core beliefs
- Use repetition and reinforcement to install new beliefs
- Engage the body and emotions to anchor the new narrative
- Bring the subconscious into conscious awareness through inner inquiry and pattern-tracking

The mind is the software of your inner technology. If you want new results, you need to rewrite the code.

Emotion: The Frequency, the Feedback, and the Fuel

Emotion is energy in motion. It's the most immediate and powerful way your body speaks to your soul—and how your soul speaks to the universe. Emotion fuels manifestation. Without it, intention is flat, energy is static, and reality doesn't move.

Positive emotion is more than a nice feeling—it's magnetic. When you feel joy, gratitude, awe, love, or inspiration, you're not just "feeling good." You're raising your electromagnetic signature, becoming a vibrational match for expansion.

But this doesn't mean you should bypass or suppress so-called "negative" emotions. Quite the opposite. Fear, grief, anger, shame—these are not blocks in themselves. They are **signposts**, calling your attention to what needs healing, reclaiming, or releasing.

True emotional power comes not from denial but from **emotional fluency**. Can you feel without being hijacked? Can you name the emotion, allow it to move, and let it teach you?

Emotional coherence is the **bridge between thought and manifestation**. It turns ideas into energetic reality. It brings heart and mind into harmony, allowing the field around you to organize in response to your signal.

Practices for emotional coherence include:

- Emotional tracking and journaling
- Heart-centered breathing
- EFT (Emotional Freedom Technique)
- Inner child work and somatic release

Your emotions are not weaknesses. They are your **fuel and feedback system**. Ignore them, and your manifestation power becomes erratic. Honor them, and you become a master of your frequency.

Intention: The Blueprint of Creation

The intention is not wishful thinking. It is the focused alignment of will and purpose. It is clarity made active. Where attention goes, energy flows—but only if that attention is anchored in **clean, consistent, and clear** intent.

Think of intention as the **architectural blueprint** of your reality. A vague idea ("I want abundance") doesn't carry enough structure to collapse possibility into form. A well-defined intention ("I welcome aligned financial opportunities that allow me to serve and thrive") becomes a **magnetic field** around which reality begins to crystallize.

For an intention to be effective, it must be:

- **Clear**: It speaks in specific, emotional language.
- **Clean**: It's not entangled in fear, shame, or inner conflict.
- **Consistent**: It is repeated, honored, and felt over time.

Most failed manifestations stem from split or contradictory intentions. You might say, "I want a loving relationship," but carry an unresolved wound that believes "I'll be abandoned again." The result? Mixed signals—and no movement.

To set potent intentions:

- Write them in present-tense, emotionally charged language
- Pair them with elevated emotion
- Revisit and reinforce them through ritual or journaling
- Clear any subconscious resistance through shadow work or inquiry

Intention is the **compass of your manifestation journey**. Without it, you drift. With it, you direct reality.

Energy: The Field That Responds to You

You are not a static being—you are a dynamic, vibrating energy system constantly interacting with the quantum field. Every thought, breath, word, posture, and feeling emits a signal. That signal is what the universe responds to—not your desires, but your **vibrational state**.

When your energy is scattered, anxious, or depleted, your field sends a distorted signal. Manifestation becomes slow, inconsistent, or blocked. When your energy is grounded, coherent, and aligned, manifestation becomes **fluid and responsive**.

You don't just "have" energy. You are energy. And how you care for your body, mind, and soul directly impacts your frequency.

Daily influences on your energy include:

- **Breath**: Are you shallow breathing in stress, or breathing deeply in awareness?
- **Movement**: Are you stagnant or in flow? Your body tells the field how alive you are.
- **Sleep and nutrition**: Physical vitality affects spiritual receptivity.
- **Environment and relationships**: Every space and person carries a field that can raise or lower yours.

To raise your energy field and optimize manifestation:

- Practice grounding (walking barefoot on earth, being in nature)
- Engage in movement that opens your body and joy (dance, yoga, qigong)
- Use sound as medicine (chanting, mantras, healing music)

- Protect your space with intention, decluttering, and energetic boundaries

A strong energy field is like a clear radio signal. The clearer it is, the more precisely your reality tunes in.

Putting It All Together: A Living Portal

When the **mind** is deprogrammed and focused, the **emotions** are coherent and flowing, the **intention** is pure and anchored, and the **energy** is strong and directed—**you become a living portal**. This is not a metaphor. It is physics. Consciousness collapses probability into matter.

Your inner gateway is not a one-time switch. It is a living interface between your deepest self and the universe. It breathes with your awareness. It responds to your integrity.

Imagine this state:

- Your mind is clear and not ruled by outdated narratives.
- Your emotions flow freely, but don't destabilize you.
- Your intention is alive in every thought and choice.
- Your energy is coherent, magnetic, and embodied.

This is what manifestation truly requires. Not tricks. Not hacks. **Alignment.** When you reach this state, life begins to respond—not randomly, but precisely. You become the signal.

You don't manifest by chasing. You manifest by **becoming**.

Chapter 6: How Trauma Blocks the Gateway

To understand manifestation in its full power, we must confront the invisible wall that stands between you and your creative essence: trauma. Not just the extreme or overt events, but the quiet, unresolved impressions that live in the body, the nervous system, and the unconscious mind. Trauma is the energy of what was too much, too fast, or too soon—what you couldn't process at the time, so your system buried it to protect you.

But energy never disappears. It gets stored, waiting for integration. And as long as trauma remains unprocessed, it subtly programs your frequency, your choices, and your expectations. Trauma doesn't just block joy—it blocks coherence. It clouds your ability to connect with the field. It distorts the signal you send out. And thus, it becomes the silent architect of your manifested reality.

This is not about blame. This is about liberation. To fully activate the gateway within, we must illuminate the shadows that cloud it.

The Physiology of a Blocked Gateway

When the body is in a trauma response—fight, flight, freeze, or fawn—it operates in survival mode. In this state, the energy is pulled inward. The field contracts. Your heart rate increases, your breath becomes shallow, and your prefrontal cortex—the part responsible for visioning, reasoning, and intuition—goes offline.

This means that when you're living from unhealed trauma, you may:

- Feel chronically anxious, scattered, or numb
- Sabotage opportunities that match your desires
- Attract relationships that echo old wounds
- Doubt your worthiness to receive

It's not because you're broken—it's because your system is trying to keep you safe based on outdated information.

Energetic Memory and the Subconscious

Your subconscious doesn't distinguish between past and present—it simply records and protects. It stores emotional memories like programs, and when triggered, it replays them without your conscious consent.

For example:

- If you were shamed for being too expressive, you might unconsciously dim your light as an adult, fearing rejection if you shine too brightly.

- If love is inconsistent or conditional, you might believe deep down that you have to "earn" your manifestations.

These patterns don't just live in your mind. They live in your field. They become your energetic baseline—the frequency that the universe mirrors back.

Trauma as Disconnection from the Self

The deepest wound of trauma is disconnection. Not just from others, but from yourself. You learn to mistrust your impulses, override your intuition, or numb your emotional truth.

When you are disconnected from your inner world, your power to manifest becomes fragmented. You may "want" something consciously, but unconsciously resist or reject it.

This is why trauma healing is not a detour on the path to manifestation—it is the path.

The Illusion of the "High Vibe Only" Culture

Much of modern manifestation teaching encourages positivity at all costs. "Think happy thoughts. Don't dwell on the past. Focus on the light." While intention is important, this bypasses a crucial truth: you cannot affirm your way out of trauma.

Ignoring your pain doesn't raise your frequency—it suppresses it. And what is suppressed becomes louder in the field. What you resist persists, not just psychologically but energetically.

The real work is not to avoid your darkness but to meet it with presence. Not to fix yourself but to feel yourself—fully, honestly, and compassionately.

Unfreezing the Energy

Trauma is frozen energy. To unblock the gateway, you must safely thaw that energy, release it, and reintegrate it. This is where embodiment practices come in. Healing happens not just in the mind, but through the body.

Practices include:

- Somatic experiencing: tracking sensation to discharge stuck survival energy
- Breathwork: using conscious breathing to regulate the nervous system
- Movement: shaking, dancing, stretching to reawaken aliveness
- Touch: placing your hands on your heart, belly, or body parts you've disconnected from

These aren't techniques—they are acts of reclaiming presence.

Rewriting the Trauma Script

Once the energy is thawed, you can begin to rewrite the story that trauma installed. This doesn't mean denying the pain. It means choosing a new lens through which to understand it.

Try asking:

- What did this experience teach me about my strength?
- How is my sensitivity a gift, not a flaw?
- What new boundaries, values, or clarity did I gain from surviving this?

You move from victim to creator. Not because the pain didn't happen, but because it no longer defines you.

To manifest powerfully, your body must feel safe to receive. Safety is not about your environment—it's about your internal state. You must teach your system that it's okay to expand, to be seen, and to succeed.

This looks like:

- Cultivating emotional regulation through daily practices
- Speaking to your inner child with love
- Creating rituals that ground and soothe you
- Choosing relationships that honor your growth

When your body feels safe, your energy opens. And when your energy opens, the field responds.

From Wound to Wisdom

Your trauma is not a curse. It is not a weakness. It is a portal. Within it lies the exact material you need to become the next version of yourself.

When integrated, trauma becomes:

- Compassion for others
- Clarity about your truth
- Power that no longer leaks

- Depth that magnetizes real connection

The gateway is not broken. It is simply blocked. And with presence, love, and courage, it can open again.

The journey of manifestation is not just about getting what you want—it's about reclaiming who you are. And to do that, you must meet every part of yourself, especially the parts you once left behind.

Because your true frequency—the one that creates worlds—is buried beneath your most sacred scars. And when you learn to hold those scars with reverence, the energy trapped inside them becomes the fuel that opens the door.

Chapter 7: Activation Through Shadow Work

Shadowwork is the sacred act of reclaiming the lost pieces of yourself—the parts you've rejected, denied, or buried to survive, fit in, or be loved. It is not just a psychological process. It is an energetic one. And when it comes to manifestation, your shadow is often the silent architect behind the reality you're trying to change.

The shadow is not evil or wrong. It is simply *unseen*. But what remains in the dark cannot be consciously directed. And so, it directs you.

The Nature of the Shadow

Swiss psychiatrist Carl Jung coined the term "shadow" to describe the aspects of ourselves we disown and push into the unconscious. This includes traits we consider undesirable (anger, envy, selfishness), but also powerful gifts we were shamed for—our sensuality, ambition, or intuition.

Over time, these rejected parts begin to operate outside of our awareness, subtly shaping our choices, emotions, and manifestations. For example:

- You want to be successful, but your shadow associates success with arrogance.
- You crave intimacy, but your shadow fears being vulnerable.
- You desire abundance, but your shadow feels guilty for having more than others.

Shadowwork brings these hidden forces into the light so they can be understood, integrated, and alchemized.

How Shadow Work Supports Manifestation

When you deny aspects of yourself, you fragment your energy. Shadow work restores wholeness. It increases your vibrational coherence and self-trust—two essential ingredients for conscious creation.

It also liberates the energy you've spent suppressing parts of yourself. That energy can now be used to amplify your intentions.

Most importantly, shadow work clears the fog between your desire and your field. It aligns your inner world so that your outer world can reflect it without distortion.

The Three Faces of the Shadow

1. **The Personal Shadow**: Formed in childhood, this includes traits you were told were wrong, unlovable, or unsafe. If you were punished for expressing anger, you may have repressed your assertiveness too. If you were praised only for being helpful, you may now equate worth with overgiving.

2. **The Ancestral Shadow**: Your lineage may have carried taboos around money, pleasure, power, or voice. These imprints can be inherited. If your ancestors were oppressed, silenced, or shamed, you may unconsciously limit yourself to staying loyal or avoiding danger.

3. **The Collective Shadow**: This includes the cultural, social, and systemic shadows we all navigate—patriarchy, racism, capitalism, and religious dogma. These shape the stories we carry about what is possible or permissible.

To manifest your fullest life, you must move beyond these collective agreements. That begins with awareness.

Common Shadow Beliefs That Sabotage Manifestation

- "If I shine too brightly, others will hate me."

- "If I receive more, someone else gets less."
- "If I rest, I'm lazy."
- "If I ask for what I want, I'll be rejected."
- "If I say no, I'll be abandoned."

These beliefs don't just live in your mind. They live in your body and aura. Shadow work is how you retrieve them—and rewrite them.

How to Begin Shadow Work

Track Your Triggers

Triggers are goldmines. Whenever you feel irrational anger, shame, jealousy, or fear, ask: *What part of me is being mirrored here?* Then ask: *What part of me have I disowned that this is activating?*

Dialogue with the Shadow

Journaling is powerful. Write from the voice of your shadow. Example:

Shadow: "I don't trust people. I've been betrayed."

You: "I hear you. What do you need to feel safe now?" Let this become a conversation. Your shadow is not your enemy. It is your wounded protector.

Name and Normalize

Speak aloud the parts you've been ashamed of. "I feel jealous. I fear failure. I want more than I let myself admit." Bringing them into language breaks the spell of secrecy. Shame dissolves in the light.

Articulate the Hidden Gifts

Every shadow holds a gift. Anger carries boundaries. Envy points to desire. Fear signals vulnerability. By claiming the gift, you transmute the wound.

Ritual Release

Write down an old belief or behavior pattern on paper. Burn it. Bury it. Tear it. Say goodbye to the version of you that needed it to survive. Honor them. Release them.

Mirror Work

Look yourself in the eye and speak the truth. Say: *"I see the parts of me I tried to hide. I choose to love them now. I welcome my wholeness."*

Signs Your Shadow Is Integrating

- Less emotional reactivity
- Greater compassion for yourself and others
- Increased synchronicity
- Clearer manifestation results
- More confidence in expressing the truth
- Deeper access to creativity and intuition

Integration doesn't mean perfection. It means presence. It means showing up with your whole self—light and dark—instead of hiding behind masks.

The Gateway Reopens Every time you meet your shadow with love, the gateway within you opens a little wider. You become a clearer vessel. The energy that once fragmented you now fuels your expansion.

Shadowwork is not always easy, but it is sacred. It is how you reclaim your power—not by bypassing the dark, but by walking through it with light.

Your shadow doesn't block your magic. It *is* your magic—waiting to be transmuted.

Chapter 8: The Role of the Heart Field

When we speak of manifestation, we often think of the mind as the command center—the seat of visualization, belief, and thought. But science and spiritual traditions alike suggest that the true epicenter of creation may lie elsewhere: the heart.

Not the poetic, romantic heart, but the electromagnetic, intuitive, deeply intelligent center within your chest. The heart doesn't just pump blood; it broadcasts a signal—one far more powerful than the brain. And when it comes to aligning with the quantum field, this signal is everything.

The Heart: Science Meets Spirit

The HeartMath Institute, a research organization at the intersection of physiology and consciousness, has conducted groundbreaking studies on the heart's energetic influence. Here's what they found:

- The heart has its nervous system—about 40,000 neurons—sometimes called the "heart brain."

- The heart's electromagnetic field is 5,000 times stronger than that of the brain.

- This field extends up to 6 feet (or more) from the body in all directions.

- The heart sends more signals to the brain than the brain sends to the heart.

In short: your heart is not just a pump—it's a transmitter, a tuner, and a regulator of your entire energetic field. When your heart and brain are in harmony (a state called **coherence**), you enter an optimal condition for healing, focus, creativity—and yes, manifestation.

Heart Coherence: The Missing Ingredient

Coherence is a state where your physical, emotional, and energetic systems are aligned and synchronized. You can think of it like a symphony: when all instruments are in tune, the music is beautiful. When they're not, the sound is jarring.

When your heart is coherent, your thoughts become clearer, your nervous system calms and your energy field becomes more stable. In this state, your intentions become more potent because they are backed by emotional congruence.

You can't fake coherence. The universe, like any good instrument, responds to what's being played—not what's being mimed.

The Heart as Portal

Ancient traditions also saw the heart as more than an organ. In Egyptian mysticism, the heart was the seat of the soul. In Chinese medicine, the heart houses the *Shen*—your spirit. In Christianity, the "sacred heart" is depicted as the flame of divine love.

The heart is consistently seen as the meeting point between the human and the divine. It is the bridge, the compass, and the altar. In manifestation, it becomes the **gateway within the gateway**—the point of access to the field where energy becomes matter.

Why the Heart Is Crucial for Manifestation

1. **It anchors emotion.** While the brain may imagine the outcome, the heart *feels* it. And the feeling is the fuel of manifestation.

2. **It regulates belief.** The heart picks up on the dissonance between your desire and your belief. If your mind says, "I want this," but your heart says, "I don't feel safe having it," the manifestation falters.

3. **It amplifies resonance.** Manifestation isn't about forcing—it's about resonating. The heart's electromagnetic field broadcasts your dominant frequency. When that frequency is coherent, aligned, and whole, it becomes magnetic.

How to Cultivate Heart Coherence

1. **Heart-Focused Breathing**

    - Close your eyes and bring your attention to the space around your heart.

    - Breathe slowly and deeply, as if your breath is moving in and out through your chest.

    - Inhale for 5 counts, exhale for 5 counts. Do this for 2–5 minutes.

2. **Elevated Emotion Practice**

    - As you breathe, bring up a memory that made you feel deep gratitude, love, or joy.

    - Let that emotion fill your chest, expanding with every breath.

    - Imagine this emotion as a color or light radiating from your heart.

3. **Coherent Intention Setting**

    - After reaching a state of heart-centered calm, speak or visualize your intention.

    - Anchor the feeling of already having it. Let your heart broadcast not a request—but a recognition.

4. **Daily Heart Rituals**

    - Place your hand on your heart and speak lovingly to yourself.

    - Write gratitude each morning—not just for what is, but for what is *becoming*.

    - Visualize your future self and let them speak back to you from the heart.

The Role of the Heart in Shadow and Healing

The heart doesn't only radiate light—it also stores pain. Emotional wounds often live here. Betrayals, grief, rejection—all of these can constrict the heart field and create energetic blockages.

That's why heart-opening is both a joy and a challenge. It requires vulnerability. Forgiveness. Trust. But once the heart softens, manifestation flows naturally. Because now, your field is clear, strong, and aligned.

Signs Your Heart Field Is Activated

- You feel calm even when external circumstances are uncertain.
- You are more compassionate with yourself and others.
- You feel deeply connected to your vision and mission.
- You notice synchronicities increasing.
- Your manifestations come with greater ease and clarity.

The Heart-Field Connection to the Quantum

In quantum physics, we know that observation influences outcomes. But what's doing the "observing"? Not just the mind—it's your *conscious awareness*, which includes the energy of your heart.

The heart doesn't just witness reality—it participates in it. It codes your desire with emotion, sends it into the field, and receives feedback in the form of intuition, signs, and opportunities.

This is why the heart is not only powerful—it is essential:

- Your heart emits a powerful electromagnetic signal that shapes your field.

- When your heart and mind are in coherence, your energy becomes magnetic.
- Heart-centered manifestation is not about effort—it's about alignment.
- Emotions like gratitude, love, and awe open the heart field.
- Practices like breathwork, visualization, and intentional feeling cultivate coherence.

Part III: Practical Gateway Activation

Chapter 9: Energy Alignment in 3 Levels: Body, Mind, Spirit

You are not just a body. You are not just a mind. You are not even just a soul. You are a multidimensional being—a living interface between matter and energy, thought and intention, spirit, and form. And if you want to manifest with precision and power, you must align all levels of your being.

Energy alignment is the practice of harmonizing your **body**, **mind**, and **spirit** so they resonate in the same frequency as what you desire. Think of it like tuning an instrument. If one string is off, the music won't sound right. If your body is anxious, your mind is doubtful, and your spirit is disconnected, your signal to the universe will be fractured.

True manifestation flows when all parts of you are saying the same thing.

Level 1: The Body – The Vessel of Vibration

Your body is your interface with physical reality. It is the antenna through which you receive and send signals. But more than that, it stores the imprints of your experiences, emotions, and beliefs.

When your body is tense, fatigued, or disassociated, your energy is scattered. But when your body is grounded, relaxed, and present, your manifestation energy becomes potent.

Practices for Body-Level Alignment:

1. **Movement** – Daily, intentional movement clears stagnant energy and raises your vibration. This doesn't have to be intense exercise. Try yoga, walking barefoot, dancing, or intuitive stretching.
2. **Breathwork** – Your breath is the bridge between your conscious and unconscious. Conscious breathing patterns (like box breathing, 4-7-8 breath, or

the Wim Hof method) oxygenate the body, release trauma, and reprogram your nervous system.

3. **Hydration and Nourishment** – Water holds memory and supports energetic flow. Eat foods that feel alive. The cleaner your fuel, the clearer your field.

4. **Rest and Sleep** – Manifestation doesn't happen through burnout. Restoration aligns your field to receive. Deep rest supports the subconscious reprogramming necessary for energetic upgrades.

5. **Somatic Awareness** – Take moments throughout the day to scan your body. Where are you holding tension? What emotions are you ignoring? Presence brings power.

Signs of Body Alignment:

- You feel grounded and energized
- You experience fewer cravings or compulsions
- Your body feels safe, open, and strong
- You can take aligned action without force

Level 2: The Mind – The Narrative Maker

Your mind is your lens. It frames your experiences and shapes your interpretation of reality. But it is also programmable. Your thoughts become your beliefs, and your beliefs create your energetic signature.

Alignment at the mind level means:

- Choosing thoughts that support your expansion
- Releasing mental loops of fear, judgment, or doubt
- Focusing your attention deliberately

Practices for Mind-Level Alignment:

1. **Meditation** – Daily stillness helps you become the observer of your thoughts instead of the prisoner of them. Mindfulness creates mental spaciousness.

2. **Journaling** – Use prompts to clear limiting beliefs. Ask yourself: *What story am I telling about this situation? Is it true? Who would I be without it?*

3. **Affirmations (with feeling)** – Spoken affirmations work best when felt deeply. Repeat statements that affirm your wholeness and vision: "I am safe to receive." "My life reflects my truth." "I create with clarity and joy."

4. **Visualization** – Mental rehearsal strengthens neural pathways. Visualize your desired outcome not just as an image, but as a *movie you're living inside*. Involve all senses.

5. **Focus Detox** – Limit distractions. Create tech-free spaces. Unfollow media that drains you. Your attention is your energy.

Signs of Mind Alignment:

- Inner dialogue becomes kinder and more empowering
- You can focus without effort or resistance
- You feel emotionally steady and mentally clear
- Your thoughts support your intentions

Level 3: The Spirit – The Frequency Keeper

Your spirit is the infinite aspect of you. It is the source of intuition, wisdom, and creative power. Spirit-level alignment means anchoring your awareness in the higher self—the part of you that already knows your worth, your purpose, and your path.

When your spirit is in alignment, you experience flow. Synchronicities increase.

Manifestations appear with little effort. You move not from control, but from trust.

Practices for Spirit-Level Alignment:

1. **Connection to Source** – Whatever you call it (God, Universe, Higher Self), cultivate daily connection. Prayer, devotion, or even a moment of awe in nature can restore spiritual clarity.

2. **Intuition Practice** – Begin to trust your inner knowing. Ask your body yes/no questions and notice the felt sense. The more you listen, the clearer the voice becomes.

3. **Service and Soul Work** – Do what uplifts others. Align with your mission. Your spirit thrives when your energy serves a greater good.

4. **Creative Expression** – Paint. Write. Sing. Make love. Spirit flows through creation. When you express your soul freely, your vibration rises.

5. **Gratitude as Frequency** – Gratitude is not just an emotion—it is a vibrational state. Embodying gratitude elevates your spirit and opens your field to abundance.

Signs of Spirit Alignment:

- You feel guided, even in uncertainty
- You experience "downloads" or inspired ideas
- You feel connected to something larger than yourself
- Your manifestations begin to feel effortless

The Harmony of All Three

When body, mind, and spirit align, you become magnetic. You don't need to chase outcomes—they come to you. You move with clarity and ease. Your energy speaks louder than your words.

This is energetic sovereignty.

Alignment is not a one-time achievement. It is a lifestyle. A practice. A way of living in dialogue with the universe.

Daily Integration Example:

- Morning: Breathe deeply, stretch, drink water, journal a few intentions
- Afternoon: Check in with your body and emotional state
- Evening: Express gratitude, visualize your next level, meditate before sleep

Start where you are. Even five minutes of alignment practice each day can change your field.

Chapter 10: Rituals to Open the Gateway Daily

The gateway to manifestation is not a one-time discovery—it's a doorway that opens wider each time you show up with intention, presence, and practice. While profound shifts can happen in a single moment of clarity, lasting transformation and manifestation require consistency. That's where rituals come in.

Ritual is the act of making the invisible visible. It is conscious repetition infused with sacred intent. Unlike routine, which can become automatic and numb, ritual awakens you. It reminds you that every moment is an opportunity to direct energy, shape your field, and align with the life you are creating.

These rituals don't have to be elaborate. Even five or ten minutes each morning and evening can anchor your vibration and open your inner gateway. What matters is the **energy** behind the practice—your willingness to be present, to feel, and to create.

Let's explore a set of simple yet potent daily rituals you can integrate into your life, starting today.

Morning Gateway Activation: 10 Minutes to Set Your Field

1. Grounding Breath (2 minutes) Start your day by sitting upright, feet flat on the floor, or touching the earth. Close your eyes. Inhale for 4 counts, hold for 4, exhale for 8. Repeat 3–5 times. With each breath, imagine roots growing from your feet into the earth. Feel yourself supported and held.

2. Heart Connection (2 minutes) Place one hand on your heart and the other on your belly. Breathe into your heart space. Say silently or aloud: *"I am here. I am safe. I choose to live in alignment today."*

3. Intentional Visualization (3 minutes) Visualize your day ahead as if it has already unfolded in the most aligned, joyful way possible. Feel the emotions of ease, clarity, support, and success. Let your body respond. Smile as you imagine synchronicities falling into place.

4. Spoken Intention (1 minute) Speak your intention aloud. Example: *"Today, I move with purpose and flow. I receive what supports my growth. I am in alignment with my highest path."*

5. Embodied Movement or Gesture (2 minutes) Move your body in a way that feels powerful and awake—stretching, shaking, dancing, or even a power stance. Let your body know: it's safe to receive, act, and express today.

Evening Gateway Activation: 10 Minutes to Integrate and Release

1. Emotional Check-In (2 minutes) Close your eyes and place your hand over your heart. Ask: *What am I feeling right now?* Let yourself answer honestly without judgment. This moment is about presence, not fixing.

2. Gratitude Reflection (3 minutes) List 3 things you're grateful for from the day—no matter how small. Gratitude is a frequency that amplifies manifestation. Speak them aloud if possible. Let your body feel the resonance.

3. Release Ritual (2 minutes) Write down or speak aloud anything you're ready to let go of from the day—stress, judgment, disappointment. Say: *"I release this energy now. I do not carry what is not mine to carry."* You may even exhale forcefully or shake it off.

4. Future Self Connection (2 minutes) Visualize the version of you who has already manifested the life you desire. See them. Ask: *What do you want me to know?* Listen. Write it down if anything comes through.

5. Sleep Intention (1 minute) As you lie in bed, say: *"Tonight I receive clarity, healing, and insight. My dreams guide me. I wake renewed."*

Optional Enhancers to Deepen Your Rituals

- **Aromatherapy** – Essential oils like frankincense, lavender, or sandalwood can calm the nervous system and raise your vibration.

- **Crystals** – Use stones like amethyst, rose quartz, or citrine to anchor intentions.

- **Candles or Incense** – Light represents clarity. Fire transforms energy.

- **Sacred Music or Chants** – Mantras and binaural beats help shift brainwaves and open heart space.

Why These Rituals Work

Because your energy doesn't start when you walk out the door. It starts the moment you wake. These rituals help you:

- Set the frequency of your day

- Prime your nervous system for receiving

- Create energetic closure each night

- Strengthen your connection with your future self

Consistency is the secret. You don't need perfect focus or perfect faith. You need presence and repetition. Energy builds over time.

Creating Your Gateway Ritual

If any of the practices above don't resonate, create your own. The key elements of any effective manifestation ritual are:

- **Presence** – You must be engaged, not distracted.

- **Intention** – Know what energy you're calling in or releasing.

- **Emotion** – Feel it. Don't fake it. Let your body be part of it.

- **Symbolism** – Use objects, words, or actions that represent your inner shift.

- **Repetition** – Let it become a rhythm, not a burden.

Signs Your Ritual Practice Is Working:

- Increased synchronicities or intuitive nudges

- More ease, clarity, or emotional steadiness throughout the day

- Clearer dreams or insights upon waking

- A deeper sense of connection with yourself and your purpose

- Manifestations begin showing up more rapidly and with less effort

Remember: Ritual is not about performance. It's about relationships. A relationship with yourself, with energy, and with the unseen forces that co-create your life.

Chapter 11: Dreamwork and Hypnagogic Manifestation

You don't always need to be awake to manifest. Some of the most potent moments for imprinting intention into your subconscious—and into the energetic field—occur just before sleep, and just as you wake. These liminal states, known as **hypnagogia** and **hypnopompia**, are neurological gateways between worlds: the conscious and unconscious, the seen and the unseen, the physical and the quantum.

When you learn to work with these states intentionally, you open a channel of communication between your waking mind and your deeper, creative intelligence. This is where dreamwork and hypnagogic manifestation come in.

These practices are not about controlling your dreams. They're about **participating** with them—inviting your subconscious into collaboration, and allowing the universal field to guide you with symbols, sensations, and insights that transcend logic.

What Is the Hypnagogic State?

The hypnagogic state is the transitional phase between wakefulness and sleep. It's that dreamy space where your thoughts begin to blur, images arise spontaneously, and your body begins to surrender. During this window, the brain shifts from beta and alpha waves (focused, alert) into theta waves (deep relaxation, pre-dream).

This is a time when:

- Your critical mind softens
- Your subconscious is more accessible
- Visualization becomes more vivid
- The veil between dimensions thins

It is a **golden hour** for planting intentions.

Similarly, the hypnopompic state—just as you wake—is fertile ground for receiving insights, interpreting dreams, and recalibrating your vibration before the world imposes its narrative.

Why Dreamwork Supports Manifestation

Your dreams are not random. They are symbolic expressions of your unconscious mind, and in many traditions, messages from the soul or higher realms. They reveal your true beliefs, fears, and desires—often more honestly than your waking mind.

Dreams can:

- Expose limiting beliefs or hidden resistance
- Confirm alignment with your desires
- Offer new solutions and paths
- Connect you with guides, archetypes, or ancestors
- Help you rehearse the future in an energetic form

When you begin to dialogue with your dreams, you increase your clarity, coherence, and creative power. You enter into a **partnership with your inner world.**

Step 1: Preparing for Hypnagogic Manifestation

Just as farmers prepare soil before planting seeds, you must prepare your field before sleep.

Evening Preparation Ritual (15–20 minutes):

1. **Wind Down the Nervous System**

    Dim the lights, turn off screens, and breathe slowly

- Light a candle or incense, or take a warm bath
- Tell your body: *It's safe to rest and receive.*

2. **Release the Day**
   - Journal briefly: What am I letting go of today?
   - Speak aloud any tensions or unfinished energies
   - Breathe them out. Imagine your field being cleared.

3. **Set a Sleep Intention**
   - Ask: *What do I want to receive or remember in my sleep?*
- Examples:
     - "Tonight I remember a dream that brings me clarity."
     - "I receive insight about my next step."
     - "I imprint my intention into the quantum field with grace."

4. **Visualize or Feel Your Desired Reality**
   - As you begin to drift, imagine your future self—calm, joyful, fulfilled.
   - Let the emotion of already having it wash over you.
   - Fall asleep at that frequency.

Step 2: Dream Journaling and Interpretation

Keep a journal by your bed. The moment you wake, before your mind kicks in, write down everything you remember—even fragments. Over time, your recall will strengthen.

Ask yourself:

- What symbols stood out?

- What emotions did I feel?
- What might this be reflecting to me?
- How does this relate to what I'm trying to manifest?

Dream interpretation is not an exact science. Let your intuition lead. Patterns will emerge. Dreams may not tell you *what* to do, but they will show you *where* your energy is blocked or aligned.

Common Dream Themes and Their Possible Meaning:

- **Flying**: Freedom, expansion, transcendence
- **Falling**: Fear of letting go, loss of control
- **Water**: Emotional states, the unconscious
- **Chasing/being chased**: Avoidance or suppressed energy
- **Doors/gates**: Opportunity, new phase, internal access

Step 3: Hypnagogic Imprinting Techniques

The moments just before sleep are ideal for manifestation because your mind is highly suggestible and your body is in a receptive state.

Try this technique:

"Drift and Drop" Method (5–10 minutes):

1. Lie comfortably in bed.
2. Begin slow, conscious breathing.
3. Focus your awareness on your heart center.
4. Choose a single word or phrase tied to your desire (e.g., *"ease," "abundance," "I am*

ready").

5. Repeat it mentally as you drift. Let it echo and fade.

6. As images arise, gently guide them to match your desired state.

7. Let go. Trust your subconscious to take over.

The goal is not control. It's an **impression**—leaving an energetic signature in the quantum field as you fall asleep.

Step 4: Lucid Dreaming and Advanced Practice

If you're ready to go deeper, you can explore lucid dreaming—the practice of becoming aware that you are dreaming, and then directing the dream from within.

In a lucid dream, you can:

- Ask guides or dream characters for advice
- Practice your manifestations in real-time
- Shift fear-based narratives into empowering ones
- Experience future realities energetically

Lucid dreaming requires:

- Reality checks during the day (e.g., "Am I dreaming?")
- Dream journaling to increase awareness
- Wake-back-to-sleep techniques (waking for 30 minutes, then returning to sleep)
- A willingness to experiment and explore

Even without full lucidity, cultivating a conscious relationship with your dreams will enhance your manifestation practice exponentially.

Bringing It All Together

Dreamwork and hypnagogic manifestation are the arts of trust, surrender, and listening. They are powerful because they involve the whole of you—not just your mind, but your body, soul, and unconscious wisdom.

You are not manifesting *alone*. Every night, you enter a field of co-creation, symbol, and soul guidance.

So begin tonight. Before you sleep, whisper your intention. Feel it. Believe it. Then let go—and dream it into form.

Chapter 12: The Sacred Delay: Why It Hasn't Shown Up Yet

In the age of instant gratification, waiting feels like failure. When we set intentions, do the work, and align our energy—yet the manifestation doesn't arrive—it's easy to assume something's wrong. We question our clarity, our worthiness, and our vibration. We start to think the universe is ignoring us, or worse, punishing us.

But what if the delay isn't a denial? What if it's sacred?

Manifestation is not magic on demand. It's not a vending machine where you insert positive thinking and outpop a house, partner, or promotion. It is a co-creative process governed by alignment, readiness, and timing—not just your readiness, but the readiness of the entire field around you.

The sacred delay is that mysterious space between desire and delivery, intention and manifestation. It is a period of refinement, not punishment. It is the universe saying, "I've heard you. Now become the version of yourself who can truly receive this."

You're Being Calibrated to the Frequency

Everything you want exists on a vibrational plane. To receive it, you must match its frequency—not just mentally, but emotionally, somatically, and energetically.

The delay is a grace period—a bridge between who you were when you asked and who you're becoming to receive it.

If the thing you want hasn't shown up yet, ask:

- Have I truly become a match for it?
- Am I ready to hold, manage, and sustain this desire?

- Is there a fear I haven't yet addressed about actually receiving it?

Your Timeline Isn't the Universe's Timeline

Your ego wants a deadline. Your soul wants evolution. The universe doesn't operate on your calendar—it works on alignment, synergy, and multidimensional timing.

There are infinite moving parts beyond your awareness. The job offer, the love interest, the funding, the relocation—they involve other people's journeys, collective energies, and unseen preparations. You are not the only piece in the puzzle.

You're Being Asked to Deepen the Signal

Sometimes delay occurs because your signal isn't strong or consistent enough. You might be oscillating between faith and fear, clarity and confusion.

The universe isn't ignoring you—it's waiting for a clear, sustained yes.

Think of it like tuning a radio. If you keep switching stations, the message can't get through. Your job is to hold the frequency—not rigidly, but with trust.

Daily rituals, emotional coherence, and intuitive action reinforce your signal. The more consistent your field, the more the field responds.

Your Attachment Is Creating Resistance

Desire is magnetic. The attachment is repellent. When you cling too tightly to your manifestation, you create energetic tension—a frequency of lack, fear, and control.

Holding the field means holding it **lightly**. Loving the vision, but not needing it to validate your worth. Knowing it's on the way, without obsessing over how or when.

The attachment says: "I need this or I'm not okay." Trust says: "I know this or something better is already mine."

Letting go doesn't mean giving up. It means letting the universe do its part.

There Are Still Lessons Unfolding

Sometimes the delay is a curriculum. It's where you learn the lessons that the manifestation would demand of you—*before* it arrives.

For example:

- You want abundance. The delay teaches you boundaries.
- You want love. The delay teaches you self-trust.
- You want visibility. The delay teaches you inner safety.

The delay is not a void. It's a sacred classroom. Ask: *What is this moment asking of me?* Then become it.

The delay can also be a mirror. It reflects your mixed signals, half-hearted intentions, or unconscious contradictions. Maybe the thing you thought you wanted isn't aligned. Maybe your soul is asking you to refine, pivot, or elevate your vision.

Don't be afraid to revisit your intention. Evolution is not indecision. Sometimes the delay exists because you're being invited to claim a truer desire.

Ask:

- Is this still what I want?
- Is it coming from alignment or ego?
- Is there a bigger, more soul-aligned version of this?

Your Growth Is the Real Manifestation

We tend to think manifestation is about the thing: the car, the relationship, the breakthrough. But it's not. It's about who you become in the process of calling it in.

The sacred delay strips away illusions. It deepens your faith. It matures your magic. It teaches you to source your worth from within, not from outcomes.

This is why so many manifestations finally arrive *after* we've stopped grasping. Because we've become whole. We've become resonant. We've become the version of ourselves who no longer chases, but receives.

So what do you do in the delay?

You keep showing up. You keep tending your field. You stay in the vibration of yes. You become the keeper of your frequency.

This is the real work. This is the real power.

And when the timing aligns, it will seem like everything changed overnight—when in truth, you were changing all along.

PART IV: MANIFESTATION AS A LIFESTYLE

Chapter 13: Living as a Gateway Keeper

To live as a Gateway Keeper means you don't just manifest occasionally—you embody creation continuously. It's not something you do in the morning before work or only during moon rituals. It's how you move through the world. It's how you think, breathe, speak, walk, love, and serve.

A Gateway Keeper is someone who recognizes that their entire life is the altar. Every thought is a spell, every action a signal, every emotion a frequency. This level of mastery isn't about perfection—it's about presence. It's about knowing that the field is always listening, and choosing to participate with awareness.

This chapter is an invitation to move beyond tools and techniques. It's about integration. It's about becoming.

You are the portal. The way you live is the offering.

The Frequency Comes First

Most people live in reaction. A Gateway Keeper lives in resonance. Instead of reacting to what is, they consciously hold the frequency of what they are creating—even when the evidence hasn't arrived yet.

You don't wait to feel grateful until you receive it. You generate gratitude as a living frequency. You don't wait for love to appear to feel whole—you generate love from your center.

This reverses the formula most people live by. They believe: "When I get what I want, then I'll feel the way I want to feel."

The Gateway Keeper lives by a higher law: "When I feel the way I desire, I align with what I desire."

Frequency is the cause, not the effect.

Energetic Integrity Becomes Your Compass

As a Gateway Keeper, your integrity is not just about morality—it's about energy. You become deeply sensitive to what strengthens or distorts your field. You begin to notice:

- Which conversations expand or constrict you
- Which environments nourish or drain you
- Which habits anchor you or scatter you

You take radical responsibility for your state, not as a burden but as a sacred duty. You protect your coherence the way an artist protects their inspiration.

This doesn't mean cutting off from life. It means choosing your inputs as carefully as you choose your intentions.

You Create Everything

The Gateway Keeper knows that creation doesn't happen in a vacuum. It happens in the micro-choices of each moment:

- How do you speak to yourself when no one's listening
- The way you prepare your food, make your bed, start your day
- The tone of your voice, the care in your presence, the way you listen

You understand that your entire life is an expression of your inner vibration. So you bring reverence to the small things. You infuse ordinary moments with extraordinary awareness.

This is not about ritualizing everything to the point of rigidity. It's about weaving magic into the fabric of your day. It's about choosing to create beauty, harmony, and alignment wherever you are.

You Hold the Field No Matter What

When challenges come, as they always do, the Gateway Keeper doesn't collapse into fear. They witness. They pause. They choose.

This doesn't mean bypassing pain. It means remembering who you are *in the middle of* the pain. It means using the discomfort to deepen your signal, not distort it.

You hold the field. You hold your frequency. You hold your vision—not as a desperate grasp, but as a sacred flame.

The Gateway Keeper becomes unshakable not because life is easy, but because their alignment is sovereign.

You Become a Beacon

When you live in alignment, others feel it. Not because you preach—but because you radiate. You become an invitation. People sense something in you that reminds them of themselves.

You walk into a room and shift the frequency. You speak and people feel seen. You create and others remember what's possible.

This is not about being better. It's about being real. Fully, unapologetically, soulfully real. In a world that teaches people to fragment themselves, your coherence becomes an act of revolution.

You Manifest Without Forcing

As you live in this state, manifestation stops feeling like a task. It becomes a byproduct of who you are. The more you align, the less you chase. The more you open, the more you receive.

You trust divine timing. You trust your process. You trust the unseen intelligence that guides all life.

You don't beg the universe. You *partner* with it. You don't wait for permission. You *listen* for direction.

Manifestation becomes not something you do, but the natural consequence of a life lived in devotion to alignment.

There's no finish line here. Living as a Gateway Keeper is not about arriving—it's about attuning. Every day you return to presence. Every day you refine your frequency. Every day you remember your power.

This is the way of embodied manifestation. This is the way of the living portal.

Chapter 14: Manifesting with Words, Movement, and Art

Your thoughts are not the only tools of creation. Your body, your voice, your hands—these are instruments of power. When aligned with intention, they don't just express reality, they shape it. To manifest through creative expression is to move beyond mental scripting and enter the realm of **embodied magic**.

We are all artists. We are all dancers. We are all poets. Not because we perform on stage or publish books, but because we are constantly composing the vibration of our lives. The question is not whether you are creating, but *how consciously you are doing it.*

When you speak with awareness, move with presence, or create from your soul, you become a transmitter. The field listens. The quantum responds. The gateway opens.

Let's explore how to harness the power of creative expression as a direct channel for manifestation.

Words as Spells

Language is one of the most potent forces you wield. Words don't just describe reality—they define and direct it. Each sentence is a declaration, and each phrase is a frequency. When you speak, you encode energy into sound.

This is why affirmations can be powerful when spoken with belief and emotion. But beyond affirmations, every word you speak carries weight. Casual complaints, self-deprecating jokes, chronic sarcasm—these aren't harmless. They're vibrations being sent into the field.

A Gateway Keeper speaks with intention:

- They speak blessings instead of curses.

- They speak solutions, not just problems.
- They speak as the version of themselves who already have what they desire.

Practices to Manifest with Words:

- Morning declarations: "I open to what serves my highest good today."
- Spell writing: Craft short, emotionally charged statements of intent. Speak them aloud or write them with presence.
- Word fasting: Spend a day or week eliminating disempowering language. Notice how your field shifts.

Words are the first form. Speak as if you are already the one who receives.

Movement as Energy Shifter

The body doesn't lie. It holds memory, story, and emotion. Movement is how the body tells the truth. It is also how the body clears, reclaims, and re-tunes.

When you move with presence, you generate a field of coherence. You anchor intention not just into your thoughts but into your cells. You signal to the universe: *I am not just thinking differently—I am living differently.*

You don't need choreography. You don't need perfection. You need presence.

The manifestation movement might look like this:

- Dancing to a song that embodies your next-level self
- Stretching while visualizing your future reality
- Walking barefoot on earth while declaring your desires
- Shaking off energy that no longer serves you

Try this: Choose one word that represents what you are calling in—freedom, love, abundance. Then move in a way that feels like that word. Let your body become the prayer.

Art as Portal

Art doesn't just express—it channels. When you paint, draw, write, sculpt, or sing, you are not only translating emotion—you are weaving energy. You are imprinting your intention into a tangible form. This makes it more real, more grounded, more magnetic.

Art can be used to:

- Encode your vision (vision boards, intention mandalas, symbolic sketches)
- Alchemize emotion (turn fear into poetry, pain into paint)
- Communicate with the subconscious (through dream-inspired images or stream-of-consciousness writing)

You don't need to be "good" at art. You need to be willing. The quality of your creative expression is not measured by how it looks—it's measured by how it feels.

Make a ritual of it:

- Light a candle.
- Set an intention.
- Create something as an offering to the field.

Let your art become your altar.

Sound and Voice as Frequency

Your voice is not just sound—it is your signature vibration. When you hum, sing, chant, or tone with intention, you activate deep layers of your field.

Sound bypasses logic. It reaches the emotional and energetic bodies directly. That's why sacred chants, mantras, and devotional songs have been used across all cultures as tools of manifestation.

Try chanting a simple mantra like "I am open" or "So it is" while visualizing your desire. Let the vibration move through your whole body.

Even silence can be a creative act when held intentionally.

Living as a Creative Channel

To manifest through words, movement, and art is to say: *My whole life is my creation.*

You don't wait for the muse. You become the muse. You don't wait for the perfect moment. You create it. When you learn to express your energy in real-time—through speech, motion, and creative flow—you are always manifesting, always recalibrating, always tuning your field.

This is not about performing for the outside world. It's about co-creating with the unseen. Every time you speak with heart, move with presence or create with soul, you become more coherent. You become more magnetic. You become more free.

Chapter 15: Sacred Sexual Energy & Manifestation

Sexual energy is one of the most potent, primal, and misunderstood forces available to us as creators. It is the life force in its rawest form—the very energy that creates new life. But beyond reproduction, this energy is a gateway to manifestation, transformation, and higher states of consciousness.

Sacred sexual energy is not about performance, fantasy, or indulgence. It is about presence, reverence, and power. When channeled with intention, it becomes a superconductor for your desires, a catalyst that expands your vibration and deepens your ability to receive.

This is why many ancient traditions viewed sexual energy as sacred. In Tantra, Taoism, mystery schools, and indigenous teachings, the body was not separate from the divine—it was a temple, and its pleasure was not shameful, but a path to awakening.

To manifest with sexual energy is not to use it as a tool of control or manipulation—it is to *merge with your desire so deeply that your whole being becomes the prayer.*

Let's explore how to awaken, honor, and direct this energy safely and respectfully.

Understanding the Creative Fire

Sexual energy originates from the sacral chakra, the energy center associated with creativity, intimacy, desire, and fluidity. When this center is open and balanced, you feel inspired, passionate, connected, and emotionally alive. When it's blocked, you may experience shame, numbness, guilt, or disconnection from your body.

The same energy that fuels physical desire also fuels artistic creation, spiritual awakening, and manifestation. That's why when you are turned on—by life, by beauty, by creativity—you are more magnetic, more alive, more open.

You don't have to be in a sexual act to access this power. Sacred sexual energy can be activated through breath, movement, intention, and self-love. It is about aliveness, not performance.

Clearing Shame and Reclaiming Sovereignty

Most people carry shame or distortion around sexuality due to cultural conditioning, trauma, or disempowering beliefs. This shame creates energetic contraction, limiting your ability to receive and radiate.

To manifest with sacred sexual energy, you must first reclaim your body as a sacred space. This requires healing, forgiveness, and permission to feel.

Begin by:

- Speaking affirmations of sovereignty: "My body is sacred. My pleasure is pure."
- Reflecting on early messages you received about desire and worth.
- Practicing non-judgmental touch—placing your hand on your womb or lower belly with compassion.
- Breathing into your pelvis and letting emotion move.

This is not about eroticism for the sake of sensation. It's about reawakening the part of you that knows how to feel deeply, desire freely, and receive fully.

Solo Practice for Manifestation

One of the most powerful ways to harness sacred sexual energy is through intentional solo practice. This is a ritual—not a release. The goal is not climax, but *circulation and amplification* of energy.

Basic practice:

1. Create a safe, intentional space with candles, music, and privacy.

2. Set a clear intention—something you are calling into your life.

3. Begin with deep breathwork and full body presence.

4. Use self-touch not to stimulate, but to awaken sensation and love.

5. As arousal builds, focus your awareness on your intention.

6. Circulate the energy—breathe it up your spine, through your heart, and out into your field.

7. At peak energy, visualize your desire already fulfilled. Let your whole body feel it.

8. Rest in stillness. Integrate. Give thanks.

This practice transforms sexual energy into a magnetic force of manifestation. It teaches you to hold more pleasure, more power, and more alignment without fear or shame.

Partner Practice for Amplification

When shared with a conscious, willing partner, sexual energy becomes even more powerful. The key is mutual intention, open communication, and presence.

Partnered manifestation can include:

- Eye gazing to connect heart-to-heart.

- Breath synchronization to harmonize fields.

- Speaking intentions aloud before intimacy.

- Touching or moving together with a shared focus.

- Orgasming together while visualizing a shared desire.

The energy created in such moments is sacred. It can be directed outward—not just for pleasure, but for purpose.

Important note: Consent, safety, and integrity are essential. Sacred sexual manifestation is never manipulative or coercive. It is a gift, a ritual, and a practice of mutual empowerment.

The Orgasmic State as Gateway

Orgasm is one of the few natural states where the mind surrenders, the ego dissolves, and the body is flooded with energy. In that moment, you are fully present, fully open, fully alive.

If you bring intention into that space—if you consciously *seed* a desire in the moment of release—you imprint it deep into your field. You send it into the quantum with the full power of your being.

Try this: As you approach climax, hold a clear vision in your mind. At the moment of release, whisper or think about your intention. Feel it ripple out from your body like a wave.

You are not just experiencing pleasure. You are broadcasting creation.

Living in Turn-On

The most powerful use of sacred sexual energy is not confined to a ritual or moment. It is learning to live in a state of turned-on presence—a life where you are attuned to joy, sensation, beauty, and inspiration.

When you live in turn-on:

- You follow what excites and expands you.
- You trust your desires as divine compasses.
- You create from overflow, not obligation.
- You magnetize opportunities, connections, and abundance.

You don't need to be in a sexual act to embody this. It's a state of openness, receptivity, and vibrant alignment.

This is not about being sexual. It's about being **alive**.

The Sacred Integration

To truly manifest with sacred sexual energy is to integrate your humanity with your divinity. It is to bring heaven into the body, and the body into heaven. It is to remember that your pleasure is not a distraction from your path—it is a *doorway deeper into it*.

You are not separate from the creative force of the universe. You are it. Every breath, every pulse, every sensation is a reminder.

Use it wisely. Use it joyfully. Use it with reverence.

Chapter 16: Relationships & Collective Reality Creation

Manifestation is often taught as a solo pursuit—your thoughts, your frequency, your desires. But in truth, you are never manifesting in isolation. You exist in a web of energetic entanglements, shared fields, and mutual influence. Your vibration not only affects your reality but the reality of everyone around you. And theirs affects yours.

When two or more people come together with conscious awareness, intention, and energetic alignment, something powerful happens. The field between them becomes a multiplier. Their combined resonance creates a third energy—a shared portal through which new realities can emerge.

This is the power of collective manifestation. Whether between partners, friends, families, or communities, our capacity to co-create grows exponentially when we unite in presence and purpose.

Understanding the Shared Field

Each person has an energetic field—shaped by their thoughts, emotions, beliefs, and embodiment. But when two people interact closely, those fields begin to synchronize. Science has shown this in studies of heart rate variability, brainwave coherence, and emotional entrainment.

What this means energetically is that when you are in a relationship—especially intimate, emotional, or long-term—you are not just managing your field. You are participating in a shared one.

If both people are clear, coherent, and aligned, the shared field becomes a potent channel for manifestation. If either person is in resistance, doubt, or fear, that energy can influence the field as well.

This is not about blaming others for your reality. It's about becoming conscious of the energies you allow into your space and the frequencies you amplify together.

Co-Creation in Romantic Partnership

Romantic relationships are among the most powerful contexts for collective manifestation. The emotional, physical, and energetic intimacy between two people creates a strong shared field. If navigated with intention, it becomes a living altar of transformation and creation.

Ways to activate collective manifestation in romantic partnership:

- Shared intentions: Set goals or visions together, then revisit them regularly.
- Conscious communication: Speak about your dreams, fears, and desires with openness.
- Energy rituals: Meditate, visualize, or breathe together.
- Sacred intimacy: Use physical connection as a space to amplify intention, presence, and trust.

Your relationship becomes a vessel—a container that holds and grows your individual and shared visions. When both partners are aligned, the energy becomes exponential.

But this also requires emotional maturity. If you are frequently in conflict, codependency, or fear, the shared field may become unstable. That's why inner work remains essential even within a collective dynamic.

Manifesting in Friendship and Community

The same principles apply beyond romantic partnerships. Friends, collaborators, and intentional communities can manifest together through shared vision, resonance, and support.

Imagine a circle of people, each holding the highest vision for one another. Each person's success is celebrated, not competed with. Each challenge is met with compassion and clarity. Each intention is amplified by the collective.

You don't need a large group. Even two or three aligned souls can create a powerful vortex of creation.

Try this with your friends:

- Host a manifestation circle: Each person shares their vision. The others hold space, reflect, and speak it into being.

- Daily check-ins: Text each other your intentions or affirmations for the day.

- Group rituals: Gather at new moons, equinoxes, or personal milestones to set and activate intentions.

The energy of a group is not just additive—it's multiplicative.

Healing and Rewriting Old Templates

Relationships also bring up the shadow. They reveal where your frequency is still distorted by old patterns: abandonment, betrayal, powerlessness, and control. These moments are not signs to retreat from connection—they're opportunities to heal and rewrite your template.

When approached consciously, these triggers become teachers. You begin to say:

- "I see where I'm projecting an old wound."

- "I notice this fear and choose to bring love to it."

- "I'm not afraid to ask for what I need or set a boundary."

This kind of emotional honesty clears the shared field. It strengthens the container for manifestation. It ensures that you're creating from wholeness, not survival.

Energetic Hygiene in Relationships

Just as you clear and align your energy, you must also tend to the energy between you and others. This doesn't mean trying to control others—it means staying sovereign within connection.

Practices include:

- Regular solo grounding, clearing, and intention-setting
- Open dialogue about energetic needs and boundaries
- Spending intentional time apart to reset your field
- Using energetic cuttings or visualizations to release old attachments when necessary

Manifestation does not require perfect people. It requires clear energy. You can love someone deeply and still recognize when your fields are no longer aligned.

The Planetary Field

On an even larger scale, we are all participating in a global manifestation experiment. Every thought, emotion, and action contributes to the collective field. This is why personal work is planetary work. When you align, you lift others. When you heal, you ripple healing outward.

The more people who live as Gateway Keepers—consciously tending their field, vision, and vibration—the more the collective begins to shift. New possibilities emerge. New paradigms take root.

Your frequency is not private. It is a broadcast. Every act of alignment contributes to the creation of a new world.

PART V: BEYOND THE DOO

R

Chapter 17: Synchronicity as the New GPS

Manifestation is not a straight line. It's not a checklist. It's not even a plan. It's a conversation between you and the field—a dance of energy, intention, and timing. And in this dance, the universe speaks to you constantly. The language it uses is not always verbal. Often, it communicates through signs, nudges, and patterns—what we call synchronicity.

Synchronicity is not a coincidence. It is a meaningful alignment. It is the appearance of external events that mirror your internal state. When you begin to pay attention, you realize that reality itself is a mirror, reflecting your energy to you in creative and often poetic ways.

Synchronicity is the universe's way of saying, "Yes. Keep going." Or sometimes, "Pause. Look closer."

When you become fluent in this language, you no longer need to chase certainty. You begin to trust the guidance that transcends logic. Synchronicity becomes your new GPS—your inner and outer navigation system for aligned manifestation.

How Synchronicity Works

The quantum field responds to frequency. Your beliefs, emotions, and intentions send out signals, and the field reflects those signals in form. But because this process involves layers of consciousness—both yours and the collective—the responses often appear symbolically before they appear materially.

Synchronicity bridges the gap. It shows you that the field is already shifting. It gives you clues that your desires are in motion and that your prayers have been received.

This might show up as:

- Seeing repeated numbers like 111, 222, or 555

- Hearing a song lyric that answers a question you've been holding
- Meeting someone who randomly mentions the exact book, teacher, or idea you were just thinking about
- Experiencing delays, obstacles, or redirections that seem oddly purposeful
- Noticing signs in nature—animals, weather, or patterns that evoke a specific feeling or insight

These are not flukes. They are echoes of your inner field—breadcrumbs pointing you toward alignment.

Learning to Listen

Most people miss synchronicities because they're moving too fast, overthinking, or dismissing them as meaningless. To receive the full guidance of the field, you must slow down and listen—not just with your ears, but with your presence.

Practice presence by:

- Taking daily pauses to ask, "What is life showing me right now?"
- Keeping a synchronicity journal—writing down patterns, dreams, and moments of serendipity
- Trusting your intuitive hits, even when they don't make rational sense
- Creating spaciousness in your day to notice what you're being shown

The more you listen, the more life begins to speak.

Following the Threads

Synchronicity is often subtle at first. A glimpse. A whisper. But when you follow it, it grows louder. The field begins to reward your attention with deeper clarity.

This is what it means to follow the threads. One insight leads to a conversation. That conversation leads to a book. That book sparks an idea. That idea leads to a decision. That decision leads to a breakthrough.

You don't need to know the whole path. You only need to follow the next invitation.

This cultivates trust in a living, responsive universe. You stop forcing things to happen and instead partner with what want to happen through you.

Signs vs. Tests

Not every synchronicity is a green light. Some signs are invitations. Some are mirrors. Some are tests.

A test is not punishment—it's a refinement. It asks: Have you chosen? Are you still in the old pattern? Are you ready to receive what you've asked for?

Common tests include:

- Opportunities that mimic your desire but come from fear
- Relationships that reflect your past self, not your future self
- Delays that ask you to deepen your faith

When you meet these with awareness, you evolve. The test becomes a portal. You show the field: I choose alignment over-familiarity. I choose truth over comfort.

Synchronicity as a Mirror

Every synchronicity is also a reflection. It reveals your dominant vibration. When you see patterns of chaos, lack, or conflict, don't shame yourself—observe. What in you is being brought to light?

When you see patterns of grace, flow, and beauty, celebrate. You are aligning. You are receiving the echo of your expansion.

Either way, synchronicity is feedback. Not to judge, but to inform.

Collaborating with the Field

You don't have to wait passively for signs. You can ask. You can co-create. The field is alive, and it responds to your curiosity.

Try this:

- Ask a clear question before sleep. Write it down. Look for answers the next day—in dreams, conversations, or subtle cues.

- Create a "sign dictionary" for yourself. Assign personal meanings to symbols (e.g., butterflies for transformation, feathers for guidance).

- Invite a specific sign: "If I'm on the right path, show me a white rose." Be open, but unattached.

This is not about superstition. It's about relationships. You are in dialogue with a conscious cosmos.

When Synchronicity Fades

Sometimes, the signs go quiet. You feel like you're in the dark. This is not abandonment—it's integration. The silence is asking you to trust what you've already been shown.

Don't chase new signs when you haven't acted on the last one.

Use this time to ground. To act. To embody. Synchronicity often returns after you've taken the step you were guided to take.

Synchronicity and Divine Timing

Synchronicities align not just with your energy, but with divine timing. The universe sees more than you. It knows the timing that serves the highest outcome for all involved.

This is why you might receive signs of something weeks or months before it physically arrives. The signs are advance notice. They're calibrating you to what's coming.

Trust the unfolding. The field doesn't tease. It prepares.

Chapter 18: The Spiral Path: Recoding Your Identity

Manifestation is not about getting things. It's about becoming someone new. You're not just changing your outer world—you're changing who you are at the deepest level. This is why affirmations alone often fall flat, and why visualizations sometimes feel hollow. You cannot hold the reality you desire with the identity that created the lack. You must shift.

But this shift is not linear. It's not a simple before-and-after. It's a spiral. You revisit the same themes again and again but from a higher vantage point each time. You meet your doubts with more courage. You hold your vision with more grace. You embody more of your truth with each turn of the spiral.

To recode your identity is to consciously rewire the beliefs, emotions, and patterns that shape your self-concept. It is to stop outsourcing your power and start remembering who you are—a co-creator, a transmitter, a gateway.

Who Are You Becoming?

The first step in identity recoding is clarity. If you don't know who you are becoming, the field doesn't know what to reflect. You must give your becoming a name, a shape, a voice.

Ask yourself:

- Who is the version of me that already has this desire?
- How do they think, speak, feel, move, and act?
- What do they no longer tolerate?
- What do they trust in without question?

This isn't about pretending or faking it. It's about merging with the future self who already lives in the frequency of your desire. It's about being her now. Being him now. Being them now.

You are not waiting to arrive. You are collapsing time by becoming.

The Old Code Must Be Seen to Be Rewritten

Every identity is built on a story. That story is made of beliefs—some conscious, many unconscious. You cannot shift your life if you don't first see the script you've been acting out.

Common identity beliefs that block manifestation:

- "I have to struggle to earn what I want."
- "People like me don't get to have that."
- "If I succeed, I'll lose love or safety."
- "I'm not special enough to be chosen."

These stories are not truths. They are survival strategies. They were installed by caregivers, society, or trauma—not by your soul.

To recode your identity, you must:

1. Name the old belief.
2. Feel the emotion attached to it.
3. Thank you for trying to protect you.
4. Choose a new belief that aligns with your becoming.
5. Rehearse and embody the new belief daily.

Identity is not changed through information. It's changed through embodiment.

The Body Remembers

Your nervous system stores your past. If you want to become someone new, you must teach your body it is safe to live in a new way. This is where most manifestation teachings fall short—they speak only to the mind.

You must involve your body in the shift:

- Practice breathwork to regulate your state.
- Use somatic movement to integrate new identity.
- Ground into your senses to stay present with change.

For example, if your new identity is someone who receives it with ease, how does that feel in your body? Open chest? Relaxed jaw? Light belly? Practice holding that sensation—even before the evidence arrives.

This rewires your system to accept what you used to resist.

Repetition Creates Reality

Your brain changes through repetition. The more you think, feel, and act as your new self, the more your neural pathways reinforce that identity.

Try this daily:

- Speak a declaration of who you are becoming.
- Visualize a moment in your day as that version of you.
- Take one aligned action, no matter how small.

Momentum is more powerful than perfection.

And remember, the ego will resist. The old identity will try to pull you back into the familiar. This doesn't mean you're failing. It means you're growing. The spiral is doing its work.

Hold Compassion Through the Spiral

There will be days when you feel like you've regressed. When your triggers return. When your doubt feels louder than your vision. This is the spiral. You are not back at the beginning. You are just integrating at a deeper level.

Ask:

- What is this old emotion asking me to remember?
- How can I meet it with love, not judgment?
- What does my future self do in moments like this?

Each return is an upgrade—if you allow it to be.

The Self as Ceremony

Eventually, the new identity stops feeling like something you're stepping into and starts feeling like home. It's not a costume. It's not a mask. It's the unlayering of your truest essence.

This is what it means to live your identity as a ceremony. Every choice becomes sacred. Every thought becomes aligned. Every interaction becomes an opportunity to anchor your becoming.

You stop seeking transformation. You realize you *are* the transformation.

Chapter 19: Rewriting the Script of Reality

Your reality is a reflection—not of your wishes, but of your dominant vibration. And your dominant vibration is shaped by your beliefs, emotions, language, and identity. When you understand this, you stop asking, "Why hasn't it happened yet?" and begin asking, "What am I broadcasting?"

Reality is not fixed. It is responsive, elastic, and intelligent. It takes its cues from you—not the part of you that makes a vision board once a year, but the part of you that speaks, thinks, and feels in habitual ways every single day.

If you want to live in a different world, you must write a new script. You must choose new beliefs, tell a new story, and vibrate at a new frequency. This is not about delusion. It's about decision. It's about becoming a conscious author of your life, not just a passive character.

The Reality Mirror

Imagine that your outer world is a mirror. It shows you not just what you want, but who you are being. It reflects your frequency with precision and neutrality. If you want more freedom, you must feel more free. If you want more abundance, you must embody abundance. If you want deeper love, you must radiate love.

This mirror does not lie. It may delay, but it does not deceive. It is always giving you information—about where you're aligned, and where you're not.

You don't change the mirror by shouting at it. You change it by shifting the image you're projecting.

Belief as Creative Code

Your beliefs are the operating system behind your reality. Some are inherited, some are cultural, some are personal. Many are invisible until challenged. But all of them act as filters—determining what you see, what you expect, and what you allow.

To rewrite your script, you must question your beliefs:

- What do I believe about money, love, time, or purpose?
- Where did that belief come from?
- Who benefits from me believing this?
- What new belief would serve my highest vision?

Beliefs are not fixed truths. They are flexible codes. When you change them, you change the data your reality has to work with.

Emotional Resonance

Emotion is energy in motion. It's what gives your thoughts momentum. A thought without feeling is static. A thought with deep emotion becomes a signal.

To rewrite your script, you must anchor new emotional setpoints. Not just think differently, but feel differently. You must practice the emotional reality of what you want—*before* it arrives.

This means:

- Feeling joy before the evidence
- Feeling safety in uncertainty
- Feeling gratitude without conditions

The field responds to your dominant tone, not your occasional wish.

The Power of Language

Your words are spells. They instruct your subconscious, shape your identity, and reinforce your vibration. Most people speak unconsciously—repeating stories of limitation, fear, or resistance without realizing it.

To rewrite your reality, you must speak a new language. One of power, possibility, and precision.

Upgrade your script by:

- Replacing "I'm trying" with "I'm choosing"
- Replacing "I hope" with "I allow"
- Replacing "I don't know" with "I'm open to clarity"

Speak as the version of you who already lives in the desired reality. Not from ego, but from alignment.

Ritualizing the Rewrite

Change doesn't happen just because you understand it. It happens when you integrate it. Ritual can help. It gives your new script structure, repetition, and reverence.

Try:

- Morning scripting: Write a page each morning from the perspective of your future self.
- Mirror declarations: Speak your new beliefs out loud while looking into your eyes.
- Nightly resets: Before bed, reframe any limiting thoughts from the day into expansive truths.

These rituals aren't magic—they're discipline. And discipline becomes momentum.

Letting Go of the Old Script

You cannot cling to the old narrative and receive the new one. At some point, you must release the identity, habits, and environments that keep you anchored to your former reality.

This may look like:

- Saying no to things that drain your frequency
- Letting go of relationships that mirror old wounds
- Choosing actions that align with your new story—even when they feel unfamiliar

Grieve the old story if needed. But do not return to it. You've outgrown it.

Reinforcing the Field

As you write and live your new script, the field begins to shift. You'll notice synchronicities, opportunities, and inner openings. But you must reinforce it, especially in the beginning.

Your subconscious mind and your nervous system are wired for the familiar. That's why consistent practice is key. The more you embody the new reality, the more it becomes your default.

Hold the line. Speak the script. Breathe the emotion. Walk the energy. The universe is listening.

You Are the Author

You came here not to survive, but to create. Not to replicate the past, but to design the future. Every belief you challenge, every word you choose, every emotion you anchor—rewrites the matrix of your reality.

You are not waiting for permission. You are not hoping for luck. You are writing the story.

And the pen is in your hands.

Always have been. Always will be.

Chapter 20: The Real Secret: You Were the Gateway All Along

There was never anything outside of you.

No ritual, no affirmation, no secret code, or cosmic alignment could replace the truth that has been waiting beneath all the seeking: *You are the gateway.* You always have been. Every tool, every teaching, every insight you've uncovered along this path has been guiding you not to something new, but back to something ancient, something whole, something already inside of you.

The final step is not outward. It is inward. It is the full remembrance of your creative power—not as a wish, but as a knowing. This is the integration of everything. The collapse of the search. The ending of the myth that you need fixing. You were never broken. You were simply conditioned to forget.

Awakening the Inner Creator

To realize that you are the gateway is to stop outsourcing power. It is to end the cycle of giving your authority to teachers, methods, or trends. You can honor the teachings, yes—but you must ultimately become the embodiment of truth. Not in theory, but in life.

When you stand in your center, you realize:

- Your thoughts are not just reactions—they are instruments.
- Your emotions are not obstacles—they are guides.
- Your body is not a vessel to tolerate—it is a compass of resonance.
- Your life is not random—it is a direct expression of your inner alignment.

The world becomes a mirror not of who you think you should be, but of who you truly are.

Living From Essence

To be the gateway is to live from your essence, not your conditioning. Essence is who you were before the world taught you to doubt. It is the spark beneath the survival patterns, the voice that whispers, "This is who I am."

When you live from essence:

- You stop performing and start expressing.
- You stop seeking and start radiating.
- You stop hustling and start harmonizing.

Essence doesn't compete. It doesn't fear. It doesn't shrink. It expands. It magnetizes. It moves through the world with grace, even in chaos.

Living from the essence does not mean life is always easy. It means you no longer abandon yourself to survive it.

Your Frequency Is the Offering

You now understand that everything is energy—and that your frequency is the most sacred offering you can make to the world. Not your image, your achievements, or your status—but your presence. Your coherence. Your vibration.

When you walk as the gateway, you bring a new frequency to every space you enter. You speak from clarity. You love without clinging. You lead without forcing. You receive without guilt. You become a living invitation for others to remember themselves.

This is how change spreads. Not through preaching—but through resonance.

You're No Longer Waiting

Perhaps the greatest shift of all is this: you are no longer waiting. Not for the job, the relationship, the approval, the sign, or even the perfect moment. You are no longer waiting because you've remembered—you are the source.

Yes, the external will still shift. Yes, manifestations will still arrive. But you're not defined by them. You're not dependent on them. You are not withholding your joy, your peace, or your power until they appear.

You are living now. Creating now. Choosing now. Embodying now.

And in doing so, you align with everything you once believed was separate from you.

No More Gatekeepers

The era of the gatekeeper is over. You don't need permission. You don't need validation. You don't need access to someone else's path. The keys were in your hand the entire time. The portal was not hidden—it was simply buried under years of conditioning, fear, and forgetting.

Now you remember. Now you rise. Now you walk forward—not in search, but in sovereignty.

Manifestation Is a Way of Being

At this level, manifestation is no longer a technique. It's not even a practice. It is a way of being. It is how you speak, how you feel, how you walk through the world.

You are not "doing" manifestation. You are living as the manifested.

You:

- Think with intention.

- Feel with clarity.
- Act with alignment.
- Receive with openness.
- Create with joy.

This isn't about perfection. It's about coherence. Coherence is a choice you make again and again.

You Are the Miracle

All along, the miracle wasn't what you were calling in. It was you.

You—the one who dared to unlearn the lies. You—the one who stopped waiting and started becoming. You—the one who chose truth over fear, alignment over approval, sovereignty over security.

This is the ultimate manifestation: not a thing, but a self. Not a result, but a return. Not an outcome, but an awakening.

So now, take everything you've learned, and don't just remember it. Live it. Breathe it. Walk it.

Let your life be the prayer. Let your presence be the portal. Let the world witness what happens when a soul remembers that it was never missing, never broken, never lost.

You were the gateway all along. And now, you are wide open.

So create. Radiate. Expand.

And walk forward—in truth, in power, and light.

www.ingramcontent.com/pod-product-compliance
Lightning Source LLC
Chambersburg PA
CBHW072159160426
43197CB00012B/2447